UNDERSTANDING UNDERACHIEVEMENT IN SCHOOL CHILDREN

About the Authors

Komilla Thapa, Ph.D., is a Professor at the Centre for Advanced Study in Psychology, University of Allahabad. She has trained as a clinical psychologist at the National Institute of Mental Health & Neurosciences, Bangalore and received her post-qualification training at the Maudsley and Bethlem Royal Hospitals, Institute of Psychiatry, University of London. She has worked in diverse areas including altered states of consciousness, stress, and cognitive disorders. She has conducted workshops for school teachers worked with disabled children and their families and provides counselling and clinical services.

Meera Varma, is a Professor in Psychology at the University of Allahabad. Her area of specialization is developmental psychology and clinical psychology in school settings. Her seminal research work is in the areas of moral development in children, parent-child relationship, aggression and altruistic behaviour in children, psycho-social competence in children, adolescents and youth. Her research papers have been published in various national and international journals of repute.

She has authored two books : *Moral development in children, and Psychology : An introduction to psychological processes.*

Chandranshu Sinha, D. Phil. in Psychology from University of Allahabad, is a faculty at Amity Business School, Noida. He has his expertise in the areas of organizational behaviour, organization development and management of change. He has to his credit many research based consultancy assignments, training programmes and workshops for corporates/organizations regarding their OD/HRD activities. He is a recipient of the "Young Scientist Award" for the year 1999 conferred by the National Academy of Psychology (NAOP). Also, he is on the Editorial Board of Amity Business Review (ABR), the bi-annual journal of Amity Business School, Noida.

Rama Charan Tripathi, Ph.D., is the Director, G.B. Pant Social Science Institute, Allahabad and former Head of the Department of Psychology, University of Allahabad. He obtained his doctoral degree in organizational psychology from the University of Michigan and was a Fulbright Fellow at the Institute for Social Research, University of Michigan (1967-68, 1982). His research interests include intergroup relations, influence processes in organizations and human resource development and rural development.

UNDERSTANDING UNDERACHIEVEMENT IN SCHOOL CHILDREN

Komilla Thapa, Meera Varma, Chandranshu Sinha
and
Rama Charan Tripathi

Published for

Department of Psychology, University of Allahabad

by

CONCEPT PUBLISHING COMPANY, NEW DELHI-110059

Cataloging in Publication Data—DK
Courtesy: D.K. Agencies (P) Ltd. <docinfo@dkagencies.com>

Understanding underachievement in school children /
Komilla Thapa ... [et al.].
p. cm.
Study conducted in Allahabad, India.
Includes bibliographical references (p.)
Includes index.
ISBN 13: 9788180694868
ISBN 10: 8180694860

1. Academic achievement—India—Allahabad. 2. School children—India—Allahabad—Psychology. I. Thapa, Komilla.

DDC 370.152 095 42 22

ISBN-13: 978-81-8069-486-8
ISBN-10: 81-8069-486-0

First Published 2008

Published and Printed by
Ashok Kumar Mittal
Concept Publishing Company
A/15-16, Commercial Block, Mohan Garden
New Delhi-110059 (India)

Phones : 25351460, 25351794
Fax : 091-11-25357103
Email : publishing@conceptpub.com

DEDICATED TO

JANE WILLIAMS

...our friend & co-researcher

FOREWORD

It is a common perception that in our system of education a substantial number of students fail to realize their full academic potential. A large number of factors are responsible for this reality. Some of these factors are related to matters pertaining to the school practices and policies whereas others have to do with larger social and cultural institutions and ethos. Authors of this volume have analysed these factors in a meticulous way, using psychological and sociological concepts for explaining a widespread and obviously sad educational phenomenon. Although the schools studied for this analysis are all located in Allahabad, the analysis and conclusion have considerable generalizability. The kinds of problems that young people going through schooling face today in developing a positive self-concept—an important factor influencing their achievement at school—are worrisomely common, both in urban and rural settings. I am sure that scholars and teachers of education and other disciplines, such as psychology and sociology, will find the analysis presented here highly interesting, and deserving further reflection.

Anxiety and stress are common features of school life in our country, indicating a serious backlog of educational reforms, especially in the context of curriculum and pedagogic practices. National Curriculum Framework-2005, which has the approval of the Central Advisory Board of Education (CABE), addresses this fundamental issue and offers a series of remedial measures in the design of syllabus and textbooks, change in the school ethos, in administrative policies which effect the working conditions of teachers, and in the training of teachers. The present volume brings out a range of factors which contribute to negative feelings like anger, resentment, and emotional reticence. The study clearly shows that such feelings are especially intense among students whose achievement at school is lower than their potential. In a democratic order, the goal of education is to enable every student—irrespective of social background—to develop his or her capacity to the maximum. I hope that the study presented in this volume will arouse greater interest in the challenging task of improving school practices and ethos in order to make the system of education an efficient means of fulfilling the goals enshrined in the Constitution of India.

Krishna Kumar

New Delhi
Director, NCERT

ACKNOWLEDGEMENTS

The completion of the research project on underachievement was possible through the cooperation and goodwill of a number of people. The State Institute of Educational Management and Training (SIEMAT) provided a generous grant and this as well as the organizational skills of the then Director, Dr. Najma Akhtar are gratefully acknowledged. Dr. Najma Saxena and the SIEMAT research team also contributed in no small measure to this study.

Schools are often regarded as closed systems that brook no interference in their workings. We are proud to assert that some of the schools we approached for this study belied these expectations. They willingly cooperated in the investigation of a phenomenon that was as complex and perplexing to them as to us. We are indeed grateful to the school management, teachers, parents and the students themselves who formed the backbone of this study.

The planning and conceptualization of this study owes much to the expertise and insights offered by Jane Williams. Jane M. Williams was a Senior Consultant at SIEMAT in 1996-97 and accompanied her husband, John Williams, a Fulbright Professor of Psychology. She was a renowned school psychologist in Georgia. Her contribution was valuable as she had ably offered a cross-cultural perspective on the educational system and highlight how schools in different contexts contribute to underachievement. Sadly, she passed away in March 2002 and this book which is dedicated to her, also commemorates her mission to make education more child-centred and to inculcate sound educational practices.

The Department of Psychology research team was ably led by Chandranshu Sinha and Kakoli Roy. Through their untiring efforts the various sets of data required for this study were obtained. The voluminous data generated in this study was creatively and competently handled by Dr. Roomana Siddiqui. Her ability to deal with the complexities of data analysis and use it to answer research questions was commendable. In compiling the Case Studies, Sonali Jana gave full rein to her clinical and creative acumen. Sabika Abbas assisted in updating the references and did an exhaustive library search. Her painstaking efforts helped in organization of this book. In the preparation of the manuscript the help given by Pankaj Bharti and Amitabh Gupta is acknowledged. We are also indebted to Prof. Krishna Kumar for taking time out of his busy schedule for writing a thought-provoking foreword for this book.

Finally, our families, by their forbearance, patience and emotional support helped in the culmination of this work.

Komilla Thapa
Meera Varma
Chandranshu Sinha
Rama Charan Tripathi

CONTENTS

LIST OF TABLES AND FIGURE

Figure

Chapter 1

INTRODUCTION

Schools hold a central place in the "developmental agenda" set forth for children and adolescents throughout the world (Rogoff, 1990; Sameroff, 1987). Children's experiences in school have the capacity to promote developmental competencies associated with learning and achievement motivation, emotional functioning, and social relationships, and in some instances can potentiate difficulties in these aspects of functioning. School as a central context of development, can shape both academic and mental health outcomes in children. Schools play a crucial and formative role in the cognitive, emotional, social and moral development of children. The role of schools in the emergence of learning, academic and emotional problems has often been ignored. In recent years, there is a growing recognition that schools have a significant role in producing such problems. However, it is equally true that "schools can act as safety nets, protecting children from hazards which affect their learning, development and psychological well-being ... schools are crucial in building or undermining self-esteem and a sense of competence" (Kapur, 1997, p. 17).

Failure to realize their academic potential is estimated to occur in at least 25 per cent of school children. Academic underachievement is a disparity between capacity and performance in which students receive lower grades than they are intellectually capable of earning. Underachievers are students of average or better intelligence who show unexpectedly poor performance in their schoolwork. Young people who are unable or unwilling to utilize their intellectual potential typically squander educational and occupational attainments that would otherwise be within their grasp.

This constitutes a waste of youthful potential and is therefore a serious social problem.

Many children attending schools have significant academic difficulties, emotional/behavioural difficulties, or most likely both (Dryfoos, 1994; Knitzer, Steinberg, & Fleisch, 1991; Weist, 1997). According to current epidemiological estimates between 12 per cent and 30 per cent of school-age children in the U.S. experience moderate to serious social and emotional difficulties that can interfere with daily functioning in and outside of school (Institute of Medicine, 1994; Verhulst & Koot, 1992; Weist, 1997). The near-term educational costs of social-emotional difficulties in children are great: Kessler, Foster, Saunders, and Stang (1995) estimate that early onset psychiatric disorders (especially conduct disorders in males and anxiety disorders in females) are related to truncated educational attainments in about 7.2 million Americans.

The Indian Scenario

To understand the phenomenon of underachievement in the total context of the educational system in India, a brief note on the status of schools and the drop-out rate in India is warranted. This would necessitate a macro-level examination of some of the central themes and factors included in this study.

The Indian educational system is the second largest in the world after China. In 2001-02, there were nearly 0.66 million primary schools in India. Between 1997 and 2002, the gross primary school enrolment rate was 111 for males and 92 for females. The net primary school attendance rate between 1999 and 2002 was 79 for males and 73 for females. However, of the children who entered primary school, only 68 per cent reached Grade V between 1995 and 1999 (UNICEF, 2004). As pointed out by Bajpai and Goyal (2004) the quality of education provided by the public education system is low. Moreover, there is a lot of 'waste' with drop-out rates as high as 40 per cent for the country as a whole and in some Indian states the rates are as high as 75 per cent. In addition, it has been observed that teacher-pupil ratios are inadequate. Teacher motivation and teaching incentives were also low. India perhaps, has the highest rate of teacher truancy in the world.

Studies have shown that caste membership also influences the drop-out rate. Drop-out rates for boys and girls belonging to the scheduled castes and scheduled tribes are higher than average. In the case of scheduled tribes, nearly 64 per cent of boys and 70 per cent of girls drop-out before completing primary school (MHRD, 1994). In addition, the caste system also plays a role in the quality of teaching imparted. In particular, in areas where children belong to castes lower down in the social hierarchy and teachers belong to dominant castes, the social attitudes towards the former are reproduced inside schools. This further de-motivates students from education and compounds the problem of low attendance and dropping out of those enrolled.

Educational deprivation in India has two crucial dimensions: lack of schools and low quality of teaching. The latter is the outcome of a combination of a lack of infrastructural facilities, insufficient incentives for teachers and weak links between the school system and society. The low quality of the school system contributes to parental apathy towards actually sending their children to school even when most parents recognize the importance of education as a means to social and economic mobility and have strong educational aspirations for both sons and daughters. Teacher apathy was observed by the PROBE (1999) team which reported that there was no teaching going on in half the sample schools visited by them, a problem further compounded by dismal infrastructure, overcrowded classrooms and lack of teaching materials and resources.

Among the dire consequences of low quantity and quality of education are the very high drop-out rates from the primary school system and poor learning outcomes of those who are in school. One World Bank (1997) study estimated that 45 per cent of girls and 41per cent of boys drop-out before reaching Grade V. Inequities prevail. Dreze and Sen (2002) note that there may have actually been an increase in educational inequality in recent years, due to an expansion of private schools which are accessible only to children from privileged backgrounds and decline in quality of schooling provided by the public school system.

Factors in Academic Underachievement

Academic underachievement can result from many different causes. These include both socio-cultural and psychological factors. Each of these factors will be briefly discussed.

Socio-cultural Factors

Academic Motivation

For students to realize their academic potential, they must be motivated to work hard on their studies. Young people who do well in school are interested in learning, they feel good about receiving high marks and they see a clear relationship between achieving in school and realizing such long-range goals as getting into college or qualifying for a particular kind of job.

In studies comparing equally bright high-achieving and low-achieving high school students, the achievers were consistently found to show strong educational motivation and to place a higher value on school and work (Morrow, 1970). By contrast, younger people who were not oriented towards intellectual values and academic goals lacked motivation to apply themselves in school. Typically, they disliked school and did not expect any inner satisfaction or external rewards to come from doing well. Academically unmotivated underachievers were unlikely to perceive their schoolwork as related to what they would be doing later or as helping them attain long-range objectives (Hummell & Sprinthall, 1965; Schaefer, 1977).

The most recent embodiment of the motives-as-goals tradition is achievement goal theory (e.g., Urdan, 1997; Urdan & Maehr, 1995). The basic contention of achievement goal theory is that depending on their subjective purposes, achievement goals differentially influence school achievement via variations in the quality of cognitive self-regulation processes. Cognitive self-regulation refers to students being actively engaged in their own learning, including analyzing the demands of school assignments, planning for and mobilizing their resources to meet these demands, and monitoring their progress towards completion of assignments (Zimmerman, 1990).

Two general kinds of goals have been identified (Covington, 2000). Learning goals refer to increasing one's competency, understanding and appreciation of what is being learned and performance goals involve outperforming others as a means to aggrandize one's ability status at the expense of peers. The specific hypothesis put forward is that learning goals favour deep-level strategic processing of information and lead to increased school achievement and performance goals trigger superficial, rote-level processing that exerts a stultifying influence on achievement.

The school environment can also contribute to low motivation, in particular for children from lower class or disadvantaged backgrounds, for whom the school may be a hostile environment. Schools remain largely middle-class, mainstream institutions. This means that middle-class mainstream children experience a considerable overlap between their school and home environments particularly with respect to what is valued and rewarded. For disadvantaged children, discontinuities between their school and home experiences frequently alienate them from the learning process. The more the patterns of thinking and behaving they have acquired at home differ from their school values and rewards, the more likely they are to become unmotivated to achieve.

The socio-cultural discontinuities between advantaged families and the school their children attend, affect parents and teachers as well as students. The parents may have difficulty in understanding the goals and methods of the school or seeing how its curriculum will prepare their children for the future. Teachers, who are well educated and mostly middle-class, frequently lack understanding of their disadvantaged students' home circumstances and sub-cultural environment. There is a tendency for teachers to expect less of children they regard as "culturally disadvantaged" and to give them less attention, encouragement and support in the classroom than they give middle-class children (Richer, 1974; Pande & Tripathi, 1982; R. Sharma, 1985).

Such negative expectations do little to build academic motivation in minority youngsters. Research studies indicate that the more teachers praise and reward children for their academic work, the more the children will expect to succeed and the harder they will try. Conversely, fewer rewards lead to lower expectations, fewer achievement attempts and lower grades (Brookover, 1978; Buck & Austrin, 1971; Sattler & Van Wagener, 1975; Weinstein & Middlestadt, 1979). Accordingly, this study examined academic motivation and students' perception of school environment.

Poor motivation and academic failure are problems that continue to plague large numbers of children in primary and secondary schools. It is estimated that approximately 25 per cent of all 10 to 17-year-olds in the U.S. are behind their "nodal grade" in school (Dryfoos, 1990). Research has also documented a decline in children's achievement motivation as they progress from elementary into middle and high school (Eccles, Midgley, & Adler, 1984; Eccles, Wigfield, & Schiefle, 1998). Untreated academic problems in children undermine not only student learning but also teachers' capacity to teach (Adelman & Taylor, 1998). Roeser and Midgley (1997) found that approximately two-thirds of a sample of elementary and middle school teachers in Michigan reported feeling "somewhat to very overwhelmed" by the kinds of emotional and behavioural difficulties some of their students presented in class.

Psychological Factors

Psychological factors that contribute to young people failing to realize their academic potential include developmental and psychopathological states that have no specific relationship to learning but handicap academic efforts and maladaptive patterns of family interaction that produce a specific and primary non-achievement syndrome referred to as passive-aggressive underachievement.

Developmental and Psychopathological States

Several aspects of cognitive, physical and emotional immaturity can impair scholastic performance. These developmental delays occur primarily in adolescence.

Cognitive Immaturity

During adolescence, young people advance from the concrete operations towards the formal operational thinking stage that typifies mature cognition. Because adolescents grow more capable of thinking in the abstract, their schoolwork becomes increasingly geared to their assuming abstract attitudes. With each advancing grade, teachers are likely to, present material and prepare examinations in ways that call for their students to exercise formal operational thinking. This means that otherwise normal adolescents who are lagging behind their peers in cognitive maturation may be handicapped in their studies by a temporary inability to abstract at grade level.

Physical Immaturity

Physical immaturity frequently impairs academic performance by virtue of the anxiety that usually accompanies delayed or arrested growth. Delayed development of puberty generates enough dismay among adolescents to disrupt their ability to function, including concentration on their studies. Thus physiologically immature adolescents who appear young and small for their age are found to have problems with academic achievement.

Emotional Immaturity

The role of emotional immaturity in school performance has been demonstrated primarily in relation to vocational attitudes, which constitute a meaningful index of maturity level. Specifically, adolescents who are undecided about their future plans have less emotional maturity than those who are working towards specific educational or vocational goals (Holland & Holland, 1977). Available evidence suggests that the lack of appropriate long-range occupational goals minimize motivation to work to capacity and thereby contributes to academic underachievement. Among both high school and college students, achievers are more likely than underachievers to have decided on a specific vocational goal and vocationally undecided students show less work involvement and earn lower grades (Lunneborg, 1975). Uncertainty and confusion pertaining to career goals would impact on underachievement. Thus this study examined career-related worries in school children.

An associated construct, which is likely to be significant in understanding underachievement, is that of emotional balance or emotional intelligence. As conceptualized by Goleman (1995) emotional intelligence is a meta-ability that influences how well the individual utilizes his/her other skills and abilities. The notion of emotional intelligence is based on the work of Howard Gardner (1993) who in his influential book "Frames of Mind" listed seven key varieties of intelligence. These included interpersonal intelligence, which is the ability to understand other people, and interpersonal intelligence, which is the ability to form an accurate model of oneself and to use that model to operate effectively in life. Salovey and Mayer (1990) came up with a basic definition of emotional intelligence, expanding these abilities into five domains.

These include knowing one's emotions (self-awareness or an on-going attention to one's internal states), managing emotions (handling feelings so that they are appropriate), motivating oneself (the ability to marshall emotions), recognizing emotions in others (includes empathy which is being attuned to the subtle signals that indicate what others need and want) and handling relationships (the skill of managing emotions in others). It was hypothesized that a lack of emotional balance would contribute to underachievement.

Psychopathological States (Including Anxiety)

By organizing, distracting or preoccupying young people, any form of anxiety can interfere with academic achievement. Some specific patterns of psychological disturbance, including schizophrenia and depression are likely to result in underachievement. Young people who cannot think clearly or maintain a normal energy level will have difficulty in earning grades in school that are commensurate with their intelligence.

One pattern of co-occurring academic and emotional problems that can arise in educational settings involve students who show academic difficulty joined with internalized symptoms of emotional distress. Studies have shown that academic difficulty can cause subsequent internalized distress (Dweck & Legget, 1988; Weiner, 1986); and internalized distress can cause subsequent academic difficulties (Nolen-Hoeksema *et al.,* 1986). Achievement-related behavioural characteristics of such students include avoidance of academic challenges, failure to persist on difficult tasks, withdrawal from classroom activities, and poor achievement. These are all signs of learned helplessness, here manifest in educational settings (Seligman *et al.* 1984).

A second pattern of academic and emotional problems that is seen among students involves achievement difficulties that co-occur with externalized forms of distress. Such children do poorly in school, show academic skills deficits and a great deal of time off-task in learning settings, have poor peer relations, and are disruptive in the classroom (Dishion *et al.*, 1995; Hinshaw, 1992). Empirical research has shown that, among some students, academic difficulty can cause subsequent feelings of frustration, inferiority, anger, and aggression that can result in behaviour problems in and out of school (Graham, 1997).

There is some indication that symptoms of externalized distress such as anger and aggression can also cause subsequent academic problems. Angry children often show heightened fears, concerns, and attention to issues of victimization, provocation, and control by others. These heightened sensitivities distract such children from focusing on academic work and learning academic skills. If such sensitivities are accompanied by aggression toward others, such children actually create conditions in which peers and teachers are less willing to offer assistance. Inattention and lack of support can in turn precipitate subsequent academic problems.

A section in this study assessed school anxiety and its contributory role in underachievement.

Maladaptive Patterns of Family Interaction

These patterns include considerable anger that young people feel towards their parents but cannot express directly. As measured by psychological tests, interviews and ratings by their teachers and reports from their parents, underachieving adolescents seem basically angrier than equally intelligent students who are doing better in school. This anger is displayed through covert channels as snide remarks, hypercritical attitudes and smoldering resentment (Dudek & Lester, 1968; Roth & Puri, 1967).

Studies of underachieving youngsters have traced their anger specifically to resentment of parental authority that they perceive as restrictive and unjust. Low achieving high school students are more likely than their equally intelligent but academically successful peers to describe their parents as too strict and over controlling (Davids & Hainsworth, 1967; Morrow & Wilson, 1961). These perceptions may or may not reflect their parents' actual behaviour towards them, however.

These findings indicate that resentment of parental control among passive-aggressive underachievers does not represent a high level of parental authoritarianism. Instead it comes from a disparity between what these youngsters perceive their parents' attitude to be and what they would like them to be. Thus underachievers use poor academic performance as an indirect way of venting their anger and retaliating against their parents.

For such retaliation to succeed—that is, for unexpectedly low grades to serve as an aggressive act—the parents must care about their youngster's school performance to become visibly upset when it declines. Typically, then, in instances of passive-aggressive underachievement the parents will be highly concerned about their youngster's academic success and distressed by his or her learning difficulties.

In addition, parental concerns and expectations have frequently contributed to an underachiever's resentment in the first place. Common in this regard is the parents' imposition of academic goals that their children do not share. When young people feel unable to question or reject their parents' demands openly, they may utilize underachievement to frustrate the parents' aspirations and take themselves out of running for some goal in which they are not interested.

The next section will include a brief survey of researches done in the Indian context.

Chapter 2

REVIEW

In this section, a brief review of Indian studies will be presented. This review will be selective and will include only those studies, which have dealt with the variables under consideration in the present study.

In the area of achievement and underachievement (Buch, 1972) has reviewed some of the earlier studies as part of the First Survey of Research in Psychology. These studies have examined the relationship between academic achievement and a large number of factors in the cognitive, affective and environmental domains including self-concept, persistence, need for achievement, adjustment, behaviour problems, fear, anxiety, emotion, drives, values, memory and interest. High and low achievers were compared on different variables such as attitudes towards teachers and intellectual functioning. Significant studies included those of (Rao, 1963) who found that over-achievers were optimally adjusted and differed significantly from both normal- and under-achievers.

Other studies have examined the relationship between academic achievement and psychological variables such as self-concept (Shivappa, 1969), emotional tension (Sabberwal, 1967) and sense of responsibility (Rao, 1964). A.K. Srivastava (1966) studied factors related to educational underachievement. He examined different criterion variables and their utility in identifying underachievers. Two such indices were study habits and reading ability (A.K. Srivastava, 1967, 1969).

In the 1970s, the school was viewed as a social system and the classroom and pupils as subsystems. Researches now focused on intra- and inter-individual factors, as well as group factors that contributed to academic achievement (K.C. Panda, 1988). For instance, the interrelationship between intelligence, creativity and school achievement was examined and it was found that each of these variables accounts for a reasonable degree of variance in school achievement. Mehdi (1974) analyzed certain dimensions of creativity such as divergent and convergent thinking in relation to intelligence and school achievement. The observation that creative thinking abilities are related to school achievement (Kakkar, 1977) was contradicted by Contractor (1976). It was posited that using school marks as criterion measures led to these equivocal findings. Kakkar and Wahi (1978) used the Progressive Matrices and examination marks and found that verbal creativity was related to achievement. Cognitive style has also been investigated in relation to academic achievement. Murthy (1980) examined the relationship between impulsiveness and achievement and found that impulsive boys and girls did poorly as compared to the control group.

In other studies, high achievers were found to be more field-independent than low achievers (S. Sharma & H. Tripathi, 1982) and cognitive style was found to be a useful predictor of achievement.

The linkage between personality and academic achievement has also been probed. A significant study was that of Mathew (1976) who identified a group of personality factors that led to under-achievement in science among secondary school students. The facilitating variables included self-reliance, sense of personal worth and freedom, feeling of belongingness and positive relations with the family, school and community. The inhibiting factors included general and test anxiety and maladjustment. He found that the facilitating and inhibiting personality variables significantly differentiated between groups of high, normal- and under-achievers who were identified on the basis of their achievement in science and scores on an intelligence test.

State and trait anxiety has been conceptualized as motivating or inhibiting academic achievement. Dubey (1976) found that students with high manifest anxiety had greater academic success but was unable to offer a plausible explanation for these findings. Seth (1978) in a study of academic achievement and emotionality found that emotionality in both boys and girls (girls were found to be more emotional than boys) led to low academic achievement. S. Sharma (1978) undertook an exhaustive review of studies on anxiety and academic achievement. The review highlighted the fact that the relationship between anxiety and achievement was unclear and obfuscated by an intelligence-anxiety interaction. The conclusive finding was that high anxiety led to low performance both at the school and college levels and in different curricular areas.

Studies have generally demonstrated that anxiety and achievement are negatively related (e.g., Jindal & B.K. Panda, 1982), while Ganguli (1983) failed to find any difference in the math achievement of high- and low-anxiety groups. These diverse findings were attributed to the use of uncontrolled independent variables and the imperfect criterion measures used for achievement.

The motivational factors, which influence academic achievement, have also been examined. These include level of aspiration, self-concept (e.g., Saraswat & Gaur, 1979) and attributional processes. Shivarathnamma (1981) found a moderate relationship between academic achievement and academic motivation. Self-concept and achievement were found to be positively related (Garg, 1981). It was found that the adolescents' underachievement frequently resulted from a distorted perception of the self as inferior, unwanted and unacceptable.

The school as a social system has been widely investigated and school environment and school climate have frequently been the variables of choice. Studies conducted at the M.S. University, Baroda (e.g., Dekhtawala, 1978) led to the development of an Organizational Climate Development Questionnaire, which enabled the classification of school climate as being open, closed and intermediate. School climate studies conducted in various states have universally found the prevailing school as being closed. As the school system can also contribute in a meaningful way to student achievement, this finding assumes significance. In addition, studies have shown that teacher behaviour also changed as a function of school organizational climate (Sanathanam & M.L. Sharma, 1972).

Kumar (1975) examined the influence of school climate on scholastic achievement and found that the open climate was optimum for personal social adjustment but climate variables were unrelated to scholastic performance. However, Rao (1976) found that the open organizational climate was conducive for pupil achievement and teacher satisfaction.

Researches on social factors have shown that value orientation, school class membership, family atmosphere, peer group influence and teacher expectations account for variations in academic achievement (Kohli & Joshi, 1978). Chatterji (1977) investigated the pattern of school achievement in primary grades. In this study it was found that children from varying backgrounds (urban *vs.* rural) and different school (good *vs.* poor school climate) did not initially differ in their achievement and cognitive development. However, by Grade V, clear-cut differences emerged in favour of boys, children from urban backgrounds and those studying in better schools.

Achievement has also been explained in terms of educational, social and humanistic values and parental educational aspirations (S.K. Agarwal, 1977). Studies on socio-economic status (SES) have, however, produced equivocal results. While some studies have reported a positive relationship between SES and academic behaviour (e.g., Raj & Krishnan, 1980), Parikh's studies (1976, 1977) failed to confirm these findings.

The influence of the social and family environment on educational performance and mental development of children is well established. An interesting phenomenon was termed the "broomstick effect" which emerged in a study on simple and complex perceptual skills conducted by Shukla and Sinha (1974). They studied two categories of schools and found that in ordinary, run-of-the mill schools, the differences in performance were all in favour of the non-scheduled caste groups. In superior schools, the "broomstick effect" was observed wherein the differential between the two caste-groups (scheduled and non-scheduled castes) was minimal initially but became progressively accentuated with increasing age. Thus underprivileged children were increasingly lagging behind on complex cognitive tasks and this difference was marked in superior schools. This phenomenon was ascribed to greater social discrimination and isolation experienced by older scheduled caste children in better institutions (Sinha , 1982). Nair (1981) identified underachievers in terms of intelligence and performance in Mathematics. He found that underachievement was greater when the father's occupation, income, education, mother's education and caste were low and the family size large.

The impact of socio-economic disadvantage on academic achievement has been the focus of a large number of studies. Children from socially disadvantaged groups become victims of our social system twice (R.C. Tripathi, 1988). First, they lack resources and the wherewithal to do well in schools, which are basically meant for educating middle-class children (D. Sinha, 1980). Second, when they enter school they are the victims of unfavourable teacher expectations. R.Rath, A.S. Dash, and U.N. Dash (1979) found that the maximum number of Brahmin and the minimum number of scheduled caste children were classified by teachers as being good in their studies. In a significant study, Pande and Tripathi (1982) found that scheduled caste children perceived the school climate as unsupportive and their academic achievement was consequently much lower. They proposed a dynamic model which postulated that an unsupportive educational environment leads to negative motivational consequences. Poor academic motivation interferes with the development and acquisition of various cognitive skills which are required for effective school performance. This impacts negatively on the academic self-concept and reinforces the negative evaluations of teachers, peers and parents.

R. Sharma (1985) also found that social class and caste significantly influence teacher expectations about student success. He found that even in the face of information that belied teacher expectation, such as, success of low caste students whom teachers expected to do poorly, teacher expectations were maintained by teachers attributing student success to chance. This pattern of teacher attribution was internalized by low caste students, which impeded their academic development. Academic achievement was also found to be negatively affected by social disadvantage. Studies (e.g., G. Misra, 1983) have shown that the scholastic achievement of disadvantaged children is lower than that of advantaged children.

In the more recent studies, two significant trends are evident. First, some studies have focused on the school environment and organizational climate as the key determinant of academic achievement. A key study is that of Pande (1980) who endeavoured to examine the relationship between perception of school climate and attendance regularity of scheduled and non-scheduled caste children. The study showed that the school climate is perceived more positively by those who regularly attended school. School attendance also led to more positive teacher expectancy and greater peer-support. Caste, however, continued to be a significant factor with teachers expecting better performance from non-scheduled caste students. Such studies have consistently found that organizational climate had a significant influence on academic achievement (e.g., S. Singh & Saxena, 1995). Among the factors conducive to academic achievement was the nurturant leadership style of the head of the institution (Roy, Sinha & Hassan, 1994), open school climate (B.N. Panda, K.D. Sahoo & J. Sahoo, 1995) and teacher attitudes (Venugopal, 1995). The dichotomy between modern and traditional schools and its impact on perceptual differentiation, long considered a precursor to academic competence was explored by R.C. Mishra and A. Agarwal (2002). They found that as compared to Hindu subjects, Muslim students obtained lower scores and students in traditional schools scored less than those in modern schools. Different types of schools (tribal, non-tribal and mixed) were investigated by N. Mohanty (2000). Working with a large sample of 600 students, she found that school type had a significant impact on academic achievement. Non-tribal schools facilitated achievement to the greatest degree followed by tribal schools and mixed schools in that order. Psychological differentiation and academic achievement were positively and significantly related across all three groups. Kumaran (2001) categorized schools on the basis of their management type and level of academic performance (low, average and high performance based on the results obtained in Grades X and XII over a 3 years period). He also examined teacher's perception of the organizational climate of their schools and found that schools differing in academic performance also differed significantly in overall organizational climate and two aspects of teacher behaviour engaged and frustrated behaviour. Teacher behaviour and school managerial practices were found to be key variables influencing academic performance. A study by S. Verma and R. Kumar (1999) showed that there was a significant positive association between study habits and overall achievement.

The second trend discernible was the focus on identifying key correlates of academic achievement and underachievement. Among the cognitive correlates, it was found that achievers had higher mental and creative abilities (Subrahmanyam & Ramadevi, 1991) and were more field independent (Kiranmaya & Vindhya, 1996). A recent review by B. Kaur, Menon and Konantambigi (2001) reported that the modal findings revealed positive relationships between field independence and intelligence, creativity and academic achievement. Studies have also shown that the relationships between different cognitive variables may be mediated by personality variables. In a study by Chinnian and Iyengar (1984) students were categorized into two groups. Group A students were characterized by definite goals, adequate motivation, persistence, and systematic study habits, whereas group B students had the opposite characteristics and behaviours. While the academic performance of group A students was consistent with their general mental ability, this was not true for group B. Mohansundaram and Murugesan (2000) examined personality variables and found that extroverts obtained higher scores on tests of achievement and creativity as compared to introverts and ambiverts.

Motivational correlates have also been investigated. While Subramanyam and Ramadevi (1991) found high achievers to be highly motivated, Sundararajan and Selvaraj Gnanaguru (1992) found no significant relationship between academic motivation and achievement. For Class IX students, they found that boys scored higher on measures of academic motivation, but the overall achievement scores of girls were higher. In another study by Gupta, Mukerjee and S. Chatterji (1993) the main findings were somewhat different. They found that intelligence was positively related to academic achievement but not to academic motivation. Girls of both rural and urban backgrounds were found to be more motivated than boys. In a series of experimental studies, Chandra (1994, 1994-95, 1995) found a reverse trend. She consistently found that girls in general set low goals. The presence of models did not alter this behaviour though rewards were effective in modifying goal setting behaviour and achievement. Achievement discrepancy and goal discrepancy were found to be significant predictors of goal setting behaviour. In a similar vein, Angira (1994) found a higher degree of achievement motivation among males as compared to females and among subjects belonging to nuclear as compared to joint families. In their study, Rani and Reddy (1995) found fast learners to have greater academic motivation than slow learners. Using a fantasy-based measure of the motive to succeed, S. Singh (2000) found high scorers to be more intelligent, highly competitive, striving for success and having better stress tolerance. P. Verma and S. Verma (2000) used path analyses and found that control, perceived competence and self-regulation were more powerful than intelligence in academic achievement. As far as girls' achievement was concerned mothers' contribution to achievement motivation far exceeded that of fathers. Aggression was also explored in a study by R. Mukerjee and Nayar (1995). They found that aggression was related to intelligence in high-achievers and to achievement in low achievers. They also found that the groups differed in the intropunitive release of aggression.

Bissa, B.G. Singh and O.P. Verma (1992) investigated the role of emotional factors as predictors of academic achievement. They examined three predictor variables (emotional maturity, ego strength and insecurity) and found that insecurity and to a moderate extent, ego strength were predictors of academic achievement. Other related studies have reported a significant correlation between adjustment and achievement (Rajamanickam & Vasanthal, 1993) and found high achievers to be better adjusted as compared to low achievers (Chouhan & Murthy, 1994).

Trivedi (1995) investigated gender differences in the relationship between anxiety and achievement. He found a negative relationship between anxiety levels and achievement among girls and students of commerce and arts stream. However, for boys and students of science, a low and insignificant correlation was obtained. Academic stress and its correlates including parental attitudes and aspirations were studied by Katyal and Vasudeva (2001). Their sample consisted of 150 adolescents with an equal number of boys and girls. They found moderate to high academic stress in all adolescents with girls showing significantly higher academic stress and anxiety as compared to boys. Parental attitudes also differed. Mothers were authoritarian and less democratic towards girls and fathers had higher aspirations from boys.

Family environment and parental attitudes have also been treated as significant contributors to academic achievement. Representative studies include those of U. Srivastava and Chandirmani (1995) who found that students from structured and independent families showed better performance. Padhi and A.S. Dash (1994) reported a significant correlation between parental attitudes and competence scores. Ramachandran (1993) identified three levels of achievement: over-, normal- and under- achievers and found that social and familial variables discriminated between the three groups of achievers. Basantia and Mukhopadhyaya (2001) studied rural students and found significant differences between the home and school environment of boys and girls as well as low and high achievers. Multiple regression analyses indicated that academic achievement was significantly related to the home environment of students. R.K. Srivastava (1995) found that students' perception of the parent-child relationship affected their academic achievement. Several aspects of parental behaviour, such as, love, disciplinc and dominance were positively related to academic achievement whereas rejection, punishment and over-protection had a negative effect. The impact of the mother's employment on the academic achievement of students in the age range of 14-16 years was investigated by Akhani, Rathi and Josore (1999). Their main findings were that children of employed mothers experienced more loneliness but their study habits and academic achievement were not adversely affected. Devi and Kiran (2002) found that the parents of underachieving students were less involved and less supportive of their academic ambitions.

Notions of the self have also been investigated in relation to achievement. Ramaswamy (1989) found that self-image was related to achievement in high achievers but not in low achievers. Rangappa (1994) found significant differences in the math achievement of students with high, normal and low level self-concepts with the high self-concept group performing well in mathematics. Focusing on the "cognitive self", R.C. Mishra (2002) reported that the actual performance of students (particularly on cognitive tasks) was significantly related to their predicted level of performance. Students' ratings of "own competence" were also significantly related to their performance. On the other hand, Maikhuri and Pande (1997) found no significant correlation between achievement and self-concept. However, significant differences were observed in the academic achievement of the high and low self-concept groups.

Among the contextual variables, deprivation was investigated by R. Gupta (2000). She examined the effects of prolonged deprivation on academic achievement. It was found that boys experienced greater deprivation as compared to girls in both rural and urban areas. The adverse effects of deprivation on cognitive functioning and academic achievement were also documented.

Assorted variables and their relationship to academic achievement have been studied. These include innovations in instructional strategies (Arya, 2000), which positively impacted on achievement. Time orientation was investigated by N.Verma and S.Sinha (2000). They found that male achievers obtained high scores on time-orientation dimensions such as perception of sufficiency of time, structuring of time and punctuality while female achievers scored highest on the dimension of time devoted to self and other-related activities. Risk taking behaviour was examined by Daftuar, Sinha and Daftuar (2000). Using a sample of tribal and non-tribal students, they found that high-achieving urban non-tribal students showed greater risk-taking tendencies. In tribal groups however, risk-taking behaviour was unrelated to scholastic achievement.

Another noteworthy study was that of M. Sharma & Mehta (1993) who investigated what they termed as "psychological discordance" (the lack of consonance between interest and chosen curriculum). They found that students who experienced discordance had significantly lower adjustment and achievement scores in comparison to students experiencing concordance.

As evident from the aforementioned studies under-achievement is a complex problem with multiple antecedents and determinants. In this study, accordingly, a holistic approach was taken with the intention of investigating this phenomenon from different perspectives by gathering inputs, from students, their parents and teachers. Thus this study focused on obtaining different levels of information from different sources with the aim of identifying commonalties as well divergences in the perceptions of these three groups. A detailed account of the method and procedures of data collection are presented in the next section.

Chapter 3
METHOD

Objectives

This study was undertaken with the following objectives :

(1) To obtain base-line data regarding the prevalence of academic underachievement in schools. This would facilitate a better understanding of the nature and magnitude of the problem.
(2) To identify the factors (psychological and school-related) contributing to achievement and underachievement.
(3) To identify underachievers in schools using composite criteria. The aim was to develop methods and procedures for identifying underachievers using an Index of Underachievement.
(4) To demonstrate the needs for the services of school psychologists and counsellors.
(5) To obtain a comprehensive view of the phenomenon by taking into account the perspective of students, their parents and teachers.
(6) To use survey results as an empirical base for suggesting remedial measures in the form of Action Programmes and school-based interventions.
(7) To provide specific policy recommendations on educational practices in schools.

DESIGN OF THE STUDY

Pre-Study Teachers' Workshop

Prior to the commencement of the study, a workshop was conducted. The aim of the workshop was to familiarize teachers and Principals with the goals and objectives of the study and to elicit their views and insights on this problem. Several schools in Allahabad were contacted for this purpose and representatives of these schools participated in the deliberations of the workshop. Efforts were made to ensure that the diversity of schools in Allahabad city was adequately represented. Thus the participating schools included both private and government schools, minority schools, boys' and girls' schools and co-educational institutions. Besides, teachers, members of the Research team from SIEMAT and the Department of Psychology, University of Allahabad participated in this workshop. The discussion focused on the problems faced by the school in helping students to perform according to their true potential. The possible causes of underachievement were explored in small groups.

The factors, which emerged as key contributors to underachievement, were as follows :

(1) School climate including teacher–student relationship.
(2) Family background.
(3) Student motivation and emotional make-up.
(4) Home environment.

The workshop also enabled the identification of key teachers who would facilitate entry into the school system. Most of the schools volunteered to participate in the study.

Research Instruments

This study used two different conceptualizations of academic functioning, one quantitative and the other qualitative (Ames, 1987). Quantitative conceptualizations of school functioning are centred around notions of *what* students *do* in academic settings. A focus on quantitative behaviours, ones that can be judged by observers of the child such as teachers, parents or peers, is central to this conceptualization. Behaviours such as performance on classroom and standardized assessments, effort assessment and time on task, are viewed as quantitative indicators of functioning. The more children manifest such behaviours, the more academically competent they are thought to be. Researchers emphasize the importance of considering not only the quantitative indicators of what children do in school, but also qualitative indicators that assess why they do what they do. Process measures such as children's beliefs about the causes of academic success or failure, their goals, their beliefs about their academic competence and the value of school are viewed as qualitative indicators. Using the above conceptualization, this study focused on both quantitative and qualitative indicators.

Based on the review of studies and the insights provided by teachers, certain personal, cognitive and psychological variables were selected for inclusion. In this study, the intention was to investigate the phenomenon of underachievement by gathering inputs from students, parents and teachers. At each level, it was decided to tap different domains of information. For example, in the case of students, personal, cognitive and psychological variables were emphasized. In the case of teachers, their expectations and perceptions of ability were salient. Some common measures, for instance, students', teachers' and parents' perception of ability and performance were included.

The domains of information obtained from each type of respondent as well as the mode of measurement are presented in Table 3.1.

A set of three forms was developed: one for Students (Form I), the second for Parents (Form II) and the third for Teachers (Form III). These forms are included in Appendices A, B & C. The

Table 3.1: Domains of information and their measurement

Respondents	*Domains of Information*	*Mode of Assessment*
Student's Form I	1. Ability	Standard Progressive Matrices
	2. School Environment	19 item scale
	3. Academic Motivation	12 item scale
	4. Affect	20 item scale
	5. School Anxiety	8 item scale
	6. Career Worries	6 item scale
	7. Academic Self-concept	10 bipolar adjectives
	8. Perceived Ability and Performance	2 items
	9. Performance in previous examinations	Marks obtained
Parent's Form II	1. Parent's rating of child's academic and learning characteristics	10 bipolar adjectives
	2. Parent's rating of child's ability and performance	2 items
	3. Need for School Counsellor	13 item scale
	4. Parent's aspirations and expectations	2 questions
Teacher's Form III	1. Teacher's rating of student's academic and learning characteristics	10 bipolar adjectives
	2. Teacher's rating of student's ability and performance	2 items
	3. Need for School Counsellor	15 item scale

measures used in the three forms are briefly described. Items were constructed in simple Hindi with a sprinkling of commonly used English words to ensure that they were unambiguously comprehended and understood.

Form I : Student's Form

The measures for students are described below :

1. *Standard Progressive Matrices*

Raven (1960) developed this multiple-choice paper and pencil test. It was intended to be a "culture fair" test of general ability. The test consists of a series of visual pattern matching and analogy problems pictured in non-representational designs. It requires the subject to conceptualize spatial design and numerical relationships ranging from the very obvious and concrete to very complex and abstract. It consists of 60 items grouped into five series.

Norms are available for ages ranging from 8 to 65. Score conversion is to percentiles. Retest reliability and concurrent validity have been found to be high, but predictive validity coefficients against academic criteria have been found to be lower. Several factorial analyses suggest that the Progressive Matrices are heavily loaded with a factor common to most intelligence tests but spatial aptitude, inductive reasoning and perceptual accuracy all influence performance. Simple instructions were prepared in Hindi and read out to the respondents. Scoring was done following the standard procedures (according to the key) given in the Manual.

2. *School Environment Scale*

This scale consisted of 19 items. Items were selected from previously constructed scales and were revised by a panel of experts. A 5-point Likert type scale (ranging from very little to very much) was used. All the items were keyed in the same direction before they were summed up to generate the total score.

In addition, two open-ended items were included. First, students were asked to write 3 statements about what they *most liked* about their school. In the second item, they were asked to indicate the 3 things they would *like to change* in their school.

Factor Analysis of this scale yielded six factors which together explained approximately 55 per cent of the variance (See Tables 3.2 and 3.3). Cronbach alpha was computed for each of the factors separately and is reported accordingly.

Table 3.2 : Factor Analysis of School Environment Scale

Factor	*Eigen Value*	*% of variance*	*Cumulative %*	*Factor Labels*
1	4.00366	21.1	21.1	Interesting School
2	1.63962	8.6	29.7	Supportive Teachers
3	1.32238	7.0	36.7	School Image
4	1.23452	6.5	43.2	Fair Teachers
5	1.55890	6.1	49.3	Attention to personal problems
6	1.00891	5.3	54.6	Peer Support

Table 3.3 : Factor Loading of Items (School Environment Scale)

Item No.	*Item Description*	*Factor 1*	*Factor 2*	*Factor 3*	*Factor 4*	*Factor 5*	*Factor 6*
5	School is very boring	.81					
9	I feel like staying away from school	.77					
14	Teachers do not want us to ask questions in class	.51					
19	I find classes interesting	.61					
1	Teachers give us an opportunity to express our views		.70				
7	Our teachers know us personally		.58				
16	Teachers help in confidence building		.52				
18	Teachers praise our efforts		.60				
11	My school is better than other schools			.63			
13	My school has good teachers			.60			
15	Students are treated fairly in matter of discipline			.58			
3	Teachers comment on personal shortcomings of students				.58		
10	Students are punished with out cause				.68		
17	Teachers are partial to some students				.63		
6	Teachers do not understand our personal problems					.75	
8	Teachers do not pay attention to weak students					.80	
2	Students conceal their feelings from each other						.81
4	Students help each other						.71

Four items (Item #s 5, 9, 14, 19) had high loading on Factor I. These items were indicative of the attraction and interest generated in students by the school. Accordingly, this factor was labelled as "Interesting School". The Cronbach alpha for this factor was .66.

For Factor II again four items (Item #s 1, 7, 16, 18) had high loading. This factor was labelled as "Supportive Teachers" as all of them focused on teachers providing emotional support and reinforcement for learning. The Cronbach alpha for this factor was .64.

Three items (Item #s 11, 13, 15) loaded on Factor III. These items referred to the perception of their school respondents, *vis-à-vis* other schools and the pride they felt. This factor was labeled as "School image" (Cronbach alpha = .55).

Factor IV consisted of 3 items (Item #s 3, 10, 17). These items had to do with fairness in meting out punishment for violation of disciplinary codes as well as fairness in evaluation and personal relationships. This factor was labeled as "Fair Teachers" and the Cronbach alpha was found to be .45.

Factor V consisted of two items (Item #s 6, 8). The content of these items pertained to teachers giving personal attention to student. This factor was labelled as "Attention to Personal Problems" and the Cronbach alpha was .40.

Two items (Item #s 2, 4) had high loadings on Factor VI. Both items are indicative of social support provided by fellow students and this factor was labelled as "Peer Support" (Cronbach alpha = .41)

A total score was computed for the entire scale. In addition, for each factor (according to the constituent items) separate scores were computed.

3. Academic Motivation Scale

This 12-item scale was constructed in a similar manner as the previous scale. This scale was factor analyzed to determine whether it needed to be scored along several dimensions or only one, that is, to understand its dimensionality. A total of 52.4 per cent variance was explained by the four factors that emerged using Principal Components Analysis (Varimax procedure). These factors and factor loading are presented in Tables 3.4 and 3.5.

The first which was the principal factor explaining maximum

Table 3.4 : Factor Analysis of Academic Motivation Scale

Factor	*Eigen Value*	*% of Variance*	*Cumulative %*	*Factor Labels*
1	2.61490	21.8	21.8	Irksome
2	1.46397	12.2	34.0	Study Involvement
3	1.17213	9.8	43.8	Negative Motivation
4	1.03517	8.6	52.4	Striving

Table 3.5 : Factor Loading of Items (Academic Motivation Scale)

Item No.	*Item Description*	*Fac 1*	*Fac 2*	*Fac 3*	*Fac 4*
2	Studies are a burden for me	.66			
5	I enjoy those days when I do not have to study	.61			
6	I often discuss study related matters with my friends	.57			
7	I cannot concentrate long on my studies	.57			
9	I do not know when I'll be rid of studies	.70			
8	I am displeased if I am asked to do some other work when I am studying		.60		
11	Nobody has to prompt me to study		.76		
4	I do not like to read books			.75	
10	I do not like to study a subject in which I get poor marks			.71	
1	I want to get a good position in class				.81
3	I want to be thorough in all subjects				.61

variance included five items (Item #s 2, 5, 6, 7, 9) and was labelled "Irksome". Most of the items, which clustered together, referred to studies as being a burden. The Cronbach alpha for this factor was found to be .53.

Factor II consisted of two items (Item #s 8, 11). This factor was labelled "Study Involvement" as it included items, which indicated positive involvement in studies, possibly for intrinsic reasons. The Cronbach alpha for this factor was .32.

Factor III was constituted by two items (Item #s 4, 10). These items were indicative of "Negative motivation" and were accordingly labelled. This factor had a Cronbach alpha of .46.

For Factor IV, two items (Item #s 1, 3) had high loadings. This factor was labeled as "Striving" as the items referred to striving for achieving success in studies and motivation to do well in class. The Cronbach alpha for this factor was .32.

For this scale as well, a total score was computed, by cumulating scores on each items. In addition, for each factor, a total score was computed.

4. *Affect Scale*

This scale consisted of 20 items. Using the same procedure as in the case of the previous scales, the Affect Scale too was factor analyzed to determine whether it was unidimensional or multidimensional.

The Affect Scale was intended to measure the manner in which students react to various stressful situations and their emotional balance.

In recent years, notions of Emotional intelligence and Emotional Quotient (EQ) have gained currency (Goleman, 1995), and are regarded as being important in understanding performance. However, the concept, which has been explored here, is broader and draws upon values and norms for the expression of emotional behaviour in our settings. The extracted factors and factor loading are presented in Tables 3.6 and 3.7.

The primary factor, which explained about 13 per cent of the variance, included seven items (Item #s 2, 3, 4, 5, 10, 13, 17). This factor was named "Emotional Control". The dimension appears to be that of impulsivity as most items referred to losing emotional balance while facing an emotion-arousing situation. This factor had a Cronbach alpha of .60.

Table 3.6 : Factor Analysis of the Affect Scale

Factor	*Eigen Value*	*% of Variance*	*Cumulative %*	*Factor Labels*
1	2.57660	12.9	12.9	Emotional Control
2	1.95745	9.8	22.7	Emotional Reticence
3	1.40505	7.0	29.7	Empathy: Sensitivity towards others
4	1.29224	6.5	36.2	Oversensitivity or Reflexivity
5	1.15171	5.8	42.0	Emotional Recovery

Table 3.7 : Factor Loading of Items (Affect Scale)

Item No.	*Item Description*	*Factor 1*	*Factor 2*	*Factor 3*	*Factor 4*	*Factor 5*
2	Small things anger me	.49				
3	I am obstinate	.52				
4	I am amenable to reason	.48				
5	I lose control when angry	.57				
10	I retaliate in equal measure when others are nasty	.52				
13	I speak in haste without considering matters	.65				
17	I am jealous of the success of others	.44				
11	I am unable to share personal matters with others		.68			
14	I am troubled by what people think about me		.52			
7	I am disturbed by the misfortune of others			.79		
8	I am disturbed by the minor problems of others			.81		
9	I almost cry after seeing the misfortune of other				.69	
12	If others are scolded for their mistakes, I feel as if I am being scolded				.71	
18	I remain annoyed for some time and then become normal					.80
19	I keep brooding over things for a long time					.40

The second factor consisted of two items (Item #s 11, 14). This factor was labelled "Emotional reticence". This dimension involved not allowing emotional reactions to surface probably for reasons of "face" and other reasons. The Cronbach alpha for this factor was .35.

The third factor included two items (Item #s 7, 8). As the item content related to being moved by the emotions of others, it was termed "Empathy: Sensitivity towards others". This factor had a Cronbach alpha of .65.

The fourth factor (Item #s 9, 12) was named as "Over-sensitivity or Reflexivity" and had items in which emotional situations and events led to reflexive reactions. Factors 3 and 4 in this sense seem seem to be related. The Cronbach alpha for this factor was .32.

The fifth factor consisted of two items (Item #s 18, 19) and was named "Emotional recovery". The items indicate the time period for which emotions persist and the time taken by the person to recover after an emotional event. The Cronbach alpha for this factor was .21.

In addition, two open-ended questions were asked in which respondents were asked to recall a happy and sad event, recount the nature of the event and describe their emotional reactions to the event.

Total scores for the entire Affect scale, as well as scores for each factor were computed.

5. *School Anxiety Scale*

To measure school anxiety, an 8-item scale was constructed. This scale was also factor-analysed and turned out to be undimensional. Cronbach alpha for this scale was .75. The items, which loaded on the primary factor, explained about 37 per cent of the variance in the domain sampled. Only these items were used for computing the index of school anxiety. Results of the factor-analysis are presented in Table 3.8. For this scale, total scores were computed.

Table 3.8 : Factor Loading of items (School Anxiety Scale)

Item No.	*Item Description*	*Fac I*
1	The thought of examination frightens me	.29
2	I fear that I may be ridiculed in class	.40
3	I feel troubled because my parents expect results beyond my ability	.30
4	I feel scared that I will not get good marks in the examinations	.56
5	I am scared of my teachers	.37
6	I feel uncomfortable while talking to my class-mates	.12
7	I fear that I will not do as well as my class-mates	.46
8	I fear that I will be humiliated in front of others	.45

6. Career Worries Scale

To measure career worries, a 6-item scale was constructed. As in the case of school anxiety, the factor analysis of the Career Worries scale yielded one factor and was found to be undimensional (Cronbach alpha = .62).

The four items loading on the primary factor explained about 34 per cent of the variance and constituted the index for career worries. The factor loading is presented in Table 3.9. For this scale, total scores were computed.

Table 3.9 : Factor Loading for Items (Career Worries Scale)

Item No.	*Item Description*	*Fac I*
1	I am uncertain about what I will do after completing my studies	.56
2	I am not getting advice about what career to choose	.71
5	I am troubled that I may not get the job of my choice	.61
6	I do not have enough information about possible careers	.77

7. Academic Self-concept

To understand how students view themselves and their academic and learning characteristics, the academic self-concept of students was examined. For this purpose 10 sets of bipolar adjectives were generated. These adjectives referred to certain common characteristics ascribed to students and which they often used to describe themselves. These adjectives are as follows: Lazy – hardworking; procrastinator (putting off studies) – studious; not planful – planful; less bright in studies – bright in studies; less successful in studies – successful in studies; poor memory – good memory; nervous – confident; viewing self as inferior to others – viewing self as superior to others; poor in Maths – good in Maths. Respondents were given the option of adding to this list of adjectives.

Negative and positive adjectives (as marked by the respondents) were assigned scores of 1 and 2 respectively. A constant of 11 was added to the cumulated score to arrive at an Academic Self-Concept score.

A similar list of adjectives was included in the Parents and Teachers Forms. Parents and teachers were asked to indicate the adjectives which best described (in academic terms) their child/ student.

8. Perceived Ability and Examination Performance

This was measured by two items in which students were asked to rate their own ability and performance in examination *vis-à-vis* their peer group (their classmates). For this purpose a five-point scale was provided. The scale points were: much less than others (1), less than others (2), similar to others (3), more than others (4), much more than others (5).

Similar items were included in the Parents and Teachers forms, whereby the parent's and teacher's perception of their child/ student's ability and performance in examinations was obtained. The aim was to find out the individual student's subjective assessment of his/her own ability and examination performance and to compare it with parent's and teachers' evaluation for possible convergence (similar ratings) or discrepancies.

Form II: Parent's Form

1. Parent's assessment of the academic and learning characteristics of their child

This was similar to the measure of Academic self-concept already described in Section-7. Parents were given the same list of 10 bipolar adjectives and were asked to select the adjective which best described the academic and learning characteristics of their child/ward.

2. Parent's rating of their child's ability and examination performance

The two items included here are similar to the items described in section-8. Here parents were asked to rate the ability and examination performance of their child, as compared to other children.

3. *Need for a School Counsellor Scale*

This scale consisted of 15 items, which outlined the major functions of a school counsellor. Parents were asked to indicate the importance of these services in helping children with their school-related performance and problems. A three-point scale was devised with the following scale points: Less essential (1), Essential (2), and Very essential (3).

A brief description of the functions (of a school counsellor) included in the scale and the corresponding items are as follows:—

Personal counselling (being available and accessible to students and assisting them in changing dysfunctional behaviour): Item #s 1, 14.

Helping with learning-related problems (providing strategies for effective learning): Item #s 2, 7.

Assessment of intelligence and aptitudes: Item #s 3, 4, 5.

Career planning (dissemination of information and guidance): Item #s 6, 11.

Parent Counselling (for effective management and maximising potential): Item #s 8, 12, 13, 15.

Advising Teachers (to enhance instructional effectiveness and classroom management: Item #s 9, 10.

4. Parent's Aspirations and Expectations from their child

Two open-ended questions were included and parents were asked to indicate their ambitions and expectations, from their child, i.e. the professional status they hoped their child would attain. Parents were asked to list 3-4 such professions in terms of preference. They were also asked to predict the likelihood/probability of their child joining the profession of their (parents') choice and the likelihood of success.

5. Demographic Details

Information pertaining to the father's and mother's education and occupation and the approximate monthly income of the family was also obtained.

6. Study Environment at home

In this section, questions pertaining to the facilities for study available in the home, were asked. These included a separate place to study and availability of required books. Information relating to who helps the child in studies (family member, tutor) was also obtained. Finally, an open-ended question focusing on the parent's main worry concerning their child was also included.

Form III: Teacher's Form

1. Personal Information

Teachers were asked for the following information: Class and subjects taught and teaching experience.

2. Teacher's assessment of the academic and learning characteristics of their students

This was a measure common to all three forms. It was similar to the Academic self-concept measures previously described in section 7 Student's Form and further alluded to in section 1 Parent's Form. The same list of 10 bipolar adjectives were given to the teachers who were asked to select the adjective which best described the academic and learning characteristics of the individual student.

3. Teacher's rating of the ability and examination performance of the student

For each student included in the sample, the teacher was asked to rate the ability and examination performance of the student compared to other students. These 2 items have been described previously in sections 8 Student's Form and 2 Parent's Form.

4. Need for a School Counsellor Scale

The scale referred to in Section 3 (Parent's Form) was also given to teachers.

5. Academic Records

Research assistants were asked to obtain details of the academic records of the students included in the sample. The following details were sought: Total marks and percentage and marks and percentage obtained in Maths in the half-yearly examination and the previous year's final examinations.

SAMPLE

Selection of Schools

A careful selection of schools was made with certain considerations in mind. The first was to ensure representation to the different types of schools and the second concern dealt with arranging mutually convenient schedules for data collection. Schools were selected using a purposive sampling design. The factors considered were (a) private *vs*. public school (b) boys *vs*. girl's school (c) co-educational *vs*. non-coeducational schools and (d) minority schools. Thus seven schools were included in the sample. With the aim of maintaining confidentiality and anonymity of the participating schools they will henceforth be referred to not by name, but by using letter superscripts. A brief description of the schools and their defining characteristics and type (given in parentheses) is as follows: School A (English-Medium, private, co-educational school with a clear cultural and ideological identity), School B (English-medium, private, boys only, but co-educational at the college level), School C (English-medium, private, convent school for boys).

Schools D and E were minority institutions, for girls and boys respectively (Hindi-medium, private). In addition, two others schools, Schools G and F included in the sample were Hindi-Medium, Government-aided schools for girls and boys respectively.

The sample size was restricted to 50 per school for a number of reasons. The first was the nature of the study, which was an in-depth and intensive exploration of the psychological and school-related factors contributing to achievement and under-achievement. Further, the heavy course-load and the limited time available during school hours was an additional constraint. Also, as the aim was to secure different levels of information from students, parents and teachers, it was decided to limit the sample. Students were selected from two levels: Classes IX and XI. The rationale for focusing on these two groups was that at the senior school level, academic pressures and career concerns become important and achievement-related issues more salient. Further, as adolescents, they are more prone to adjustment and minor emotional problems. Also, it was easier to access these groups, as compared to class X and XII students who were preparing for their Board examinations. Thus, the final sample consisted of 350 subjects in the age-range of 12-19 years. 229 boys and 121 girls constituted the sample, which was randomly selected from schools. Details of the sample are presented in Table 3.10.

Table 3.10 : Sample of the Study

School	*Class*	*Students*	*Teachers*	*Parents*
A	XI	25	2	46
	IX	25	3	
B	XI	25	4	48
	IX	25	5	
C	XI	25	3	47
	IX	25	4	
D	XI	25	3	40
	IX	25	4	
E	XI	25	4	31
	IX	25	4	
		350	44	253

Procedure of Data Collection

The research team consisting of trained research personnel from the University Department of Psychology and SIEMAT contacted the school authorities and made arrangements for data collection.

From school registers, students were randomly selected. The total number of students in class IX (including all sections) was determined and the total number obtained was divided by 25 (the desired sample size). The figure thus obtained (nth) was the basis for selecting every nth student for the sample. For example, if the total number of students was 150, then every sixth student (following the same order of names as given in the attendance register) was included in the sample. A similar procedure was followed for Class XI students. After these 25 students had been randomly selected, they were seated in a new serial order assigned by the Research team. The Standard Progressive Matrices was first administered followed by the Student's Form.

At the same time, class teachers and Maths teachers were contacted and asked to complete the Teacher's Form. They were asked to make individual evaluations for each student included in the sample.

Finally, a Parent's Form was handed over to the student sample. The included a covering letter stating the aims of the study and requesting parents to complete the enclosed forms. Students were asked to return the completed forms in a sealed envelope to their class-teachers.

The research team re-visited the schools after a few days to collect the Teacher's and Parent's Forms and to obtain the current and previous year's marks from school records.

Chapter 4

RESULTS

Both quantitative and qualitative data were obtained from the respondents. Coding manuals were developed for coding the quantitative data. For the qualitative data, content categories were devised and the data coded accordingly. As the data from School G was incomplete, in particular information required for identifying levels of underachievement was unavailable, this school was excluded from subsequent analyses. Preliminary analyses were done to study the overall pattern of the results. For this purpose, initially, school-wise analyses was done in which the Means (M) Standard Deviations (SD), Analysis of Variance, (ANOVA) were computed and where applicable the Student-Newman Keuls procedure (Multiple Range Test) was used. These results are presented in Table 4.1.

Table 4.1 : Mean Comparisons of Psychological Indices for the 6 schools

Variables	*Schools*						*F*
	A	*B*	*C*	*D*	*E*	*F*	
School Environment (Total)	65.73^{a}	60.34^{b}	62.45^{ab}	70.76^{c}	63.41^{ab}	63.31^{ab}	6.68**
1. Interesting School	15.82^{a}	14.20^{a}	14.40^{a}	17.16^{b}	14.95^{a}	14.67^{a}	5.62**
2. Supportive Teachers	12.41^{ac}	10.50^{b}	10.46^{b}	13.36^{ac}	11.46^{ab}	9.95^{b}	9.11**
3. School Image	10.89^{a}	10.18^{a}	10.36^{a}	12.86^{b}	10.20^{a}	9.48^{a}	9.92**
4. Fair Teachers	10.75^{a}	10.02^{b}	9.54^{b}	10.77^{b}	10.65^{a}	11.96^{a}	4.59**
5. Attention to Personal Problems	6.46	6.16	7.20	6.62	6.36	7.36	2.35
6. Peer support	6.70	6.48	7.36	7.58	6.62	7.06	2.40

Continued...

Variables	Schools						*F*
	A	*B*	*C*	*D*	*E*	*F*	
Academic Motivation (Total)	46.81	44.04	44.06	44.82	45.93	45.10	1.06
1. Irksome	15.95[a]	15.34[a]	14.93[b]	16.28[a]	16.48[a]	17.08[a]	3.00**
2. Study Involvement	7.22[abcd]	6.94[abcd]	6.88[bcd]	5.96[ab]	7.46[abcd]	5.80[a]	4.98**
3. Negative Motivation	8.26	7.24	7.67	7.61	7.18	7.28	1.70
4. Striving	9.06	8.46	8.58	8.20	8.42	8.30	1.59

Variables	Schools						*F*
	A	*B*	*C*	*D*	*E*	*F*	
Affect (Total)	28.00	27.20	28.46	27.46	27.14	27.00	1.06
Emotional Control	14.14	14.18	14.40	15.18	14.67	14.79	1.38
Emotional Reticence	3.82	3.34	3.84	3.46	3.28	3.52	1.96
Empathy	3.42	3.32	3.46	2.88	3.04	3.06	2.46
Oversensitivity	3.62[ac]	3.32[ac]	3.58[ac]	2.80[b]	3.14[ac]	2.80[b]	5.24**
Emotional Recovery	3.06	3.04	3.18	3.06	3.10	2.96	.32

Variables	Schools						*F*
	A	*B*	*C*	*D*	*E*	*F*	
School Anxiety (Total)	21.65	23.76	23.18	22.96	22.39	21.95	.94
Career Worries (Total)	10.24[a]	10.16[ab]	10.89[a]	12.51[bc]	12.67[c]	11.18[a]	4.17**

Note: * $p < .05$ ** $p < .01$

Means with common subscripts do not differ significantly.

This table shows significant differences between schools on two scales, School Environment [F = 6.68, df (6,323), p<.01] and Career Worries [F = 4.17, df (6,336), p<.01]. Generally speaking students of School D tended to perceive the school environment more positively than students of all other schools, whereas students of School B had less positive views of their school.

Among the factors of this scale, 4 factors: Interesting school, supportive teachers, school image and fair teachers all showed significant differences. School D students rated their school more positively, found there teachers to be more supportive and had a positive image of their school while School A students rated their teachers as more supportive, students of School F felt their teachers were fair and impartial in disciplinary matters and evaluation.

For the Academic Motivation scale, two factors, Irksome and study involvement showed significant difference. Here School F students found studies to be a great burden and involvement in studies was significantly higher in students from Schools A, B, C and E.

For the Affect scale, oversensitivity or reflexivity elicited significant differences. Students from Schools A and C showed significantly higher scores on this aspect of emotional behaviour. Career Worries were found to be significantly higher in Schools D and E and lower in Schools A and B.

Gender differences were also examined and results are presented in Table 4.2. Briefly, these results indicate that girls perceived the school environment more positively and teachers rated their academic abilities in a more positive manner. On all the other psychological variables, non-significant and minor differences were observed.

Table 4.2 : Gender Differences on Psychological Variables

Psychological Variable	*Males*		*Females*		*t*
	M	*SD*	*M*	*SD*	
School Environment	63.65	9.48	66.48	9.25	2.63**
Academic Motivation	45.40	6.54	45.16	6.41	-.32
Affect	27.69	3.62	27.14	3.61	-1.33
School Anxiety	22.43	61.4	22.58	6.5	.21
Career Worries	16.64	4.40	16.86	4.07	.45
Academic Self Concept	15.77	2.22	15.83	2.17	.26
Academic Abilities: Teacher	14.39	3.50	16.15	3.11	3.19**
Academic Abilities: Parent	16.31	2.33	16.34	2.43	.10

Note: ** $p < .01$

Index of Underachievement

Preliminary analyses in the form of frequencies and correlations were done to identify the relevant variables which could be used to compute the Index of Underachievement.

An examination of the correlation patterns showed that this Index could best be computed by finding out the discrepancy between Actual Ability (total score obtained on Standard Progressive Matrices) and Actual Performance (percentage obtained in the previous year's final examination). The correlation between these two variables was .44 ($p<.01$).

A 5 × 5 matrix was developed, consisting of 25 cells and students were placed in each of these cells according to their level of achievement and underachievement. This matrix is presented in Table 4.3.

Table 4.3 : Matrix of Achievement and Under Achievement

		(Actual Performance) *Grades*				
	Levels	1	2	3	4	5
Actual Ability	I	N	UA	UA	UA	UA
	II	OA	N	UA	UA	UA
	III	OA	OA	N	UA	UA
	IV	OA	OA	OA	N	UA
	V	OA	OA	OA	OA	N

Note: N = Normal Achievement
UA = Under Achievement
OA = Over Achievement

A perusal of the data showed that the scores obtained on the Standard Progressive Matrices (SPM) could be arranged according to the grades given in the Manual. For example, if the subject's scores were in the range of 54–64, the grade assigned was I, scores in the range of 49-53 were treated as Grade II, scores in the range of 38-49 constituted Grade III, scores of 24-37 were placed in Grade IV and scores of 0-23 were placed in Grade V.

Percentage of marks obtained in the previous examination were similarly arranged in 5 levels. If subjects scored between 75-100 it was treated as Level 1, marks between 65-74 were treated as Level 2, marks between 56 64 were treated as Level 3, marks in the range of 50-55 were treated as Level 4 and marks in the range of 19-49 were treated as Level 5. For this Index, only those subjects were included for whom information on both variables were available. In some schools (notably School G) it was not possible to obtain information pertaining to the Academic record of subjects. These subjects were perforce excluded from the sample. The sample used for the computation of this Index was thereby reduced to 246. Patterned variables were created in various combinations based on the discrepancies between SPM scores and Examination results. For this purpose, the cross-tabulation procedure was used and the results are presented in Table 4.4. The results were interpreted in accordance with the matrix developed earlier (Table 4.2). For example, high scores on the Matrices (Grades I and II) and poor performance (Examination results at levels 4 and 5) were treated as indicators of Extreme Underachievement and were labelled as UA1. These were students who had high ability but performed very poorly in the exams.

Similarly, high scores on SPM (Grades I, II, & III) and moderate to poor performance (Exam results at levels 3, 4 & 5) were treated as indicators of Moderate Underachievement and were labelled as UA2. High to moderate scores on SPM (Grades I, II, III and IV) and moderate to poor performance (Exam results at levels 2, 3, 4 and 5) were treated as indicators of Marginal Underachievement and labelled as UA3. In other words, as the discrepancy between Actual Ability and Actual Performance became smaller, the severity of underachievement also decreased.

Other conditions examined were as follows: If the SPM scores, were in the range of Grades II, III, IV and V and Examination results were a grade higher (that is at levels 1, 2, 3 and 4), these cases were treated as indicative of Moderate Over achievement or achievement exceeding ability and were labelled as OA1. If the SPM were average to poor (Grades III, IV and V) and the performance in exams was better (that is at levels 1, 2 and 3), these cases were treated as indicative of Extreme Over achievement (OA2).

Table 4.4 : Matrix of Achievement and Under Achievement

		(Actual Performance) *Grades*				
	Levels	*1*	*2*	*3*	*4*	*5*
Actual Ability	I	24 (N)	23 (UA3)	11 (UA2)	2 (UA1)	2 (UA1)
	II	10 (OA1)	15 (N)	14 (UA3)	9 (UA2)	5 (UA1)
	III	10 (OA2)	15 (OA1)	24 (N)	20 (UA3)	22 (UA1)
	IV	-	2 (OA2)	10 (OA1)	7 (N)	8 (UA3)
	V	-	1 (OA2)	3 (OA2)	5 (OA1)	4 (N)

Note: N = Normal Achievement
UA1 = Extreme Underachievement
UA2 = Moderate Underachievement
UA3 = Marginal Underachievement
OA1= Over achievement
OA2 = Moderate Over achievement

Thus, five under achievement and over achievement groups were identified. (see Fig. 4.1). These groups were as follows:-

Group 1	Extreme Under achievement (UA1)	N = 9
Group 2	Moderate Under achievement (UA2)	N = 42
Group 3	Marginal Under achievement (UA3)	N = 65
Group 4	Marginal Over achievement (OA1)	N = 40
Group 5	Moderate Over achievement (OA2)	N = 16

Seventy four subjects were identified in whom there was a perfect correspondence between actual ability and performance. Subsequent analyses were done using these five groups of subjects.

The figure clearly illustrate that approximately 47 per cent of sample studied were placed in the under achievers group, of which about 3.7 per cent were extreme under achievers, 17 per cent were moderate under achievers and 26 per cent were marginal under achievers. The normal achievers group constituted 30 per cent of the sample. Equally significant was the finding that at least

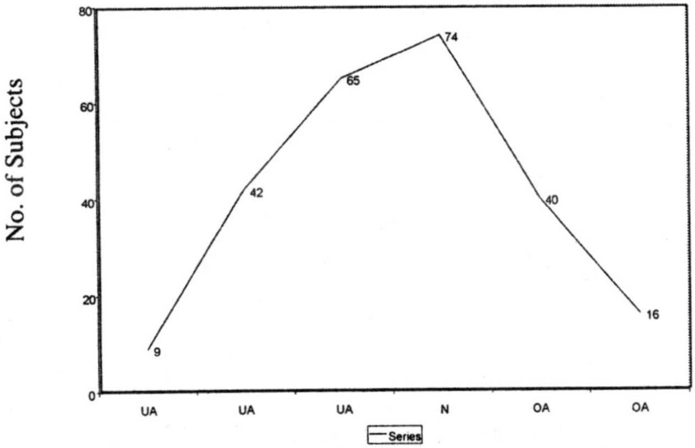

Fig. 4.1 : Distribution of Under, Normal and Over-Achievers

23 per cent of the sample had academic achievement exceeding their ability with 16 per cent showing marginal over-achievement and 6.5 per cent showing moderate over achievement.

In addition, the under achievement groups (UA1, UA2 & UA3) was combined to form a single under achievers groups (N=116). The normal achievers group consisted of 74 subjects. An over-achievers group was formed (OA1 + OA2) consisting of 56 subjects.

A school-wise distribution of normal, over– and under-achievers is presented in Table 4.5 Under- and over-achievers were further subdivided in terms of the degree of under– and over-achievement. The incidence according to the 5 levels of under- and over- achievement is presented in Table 4.6. As is clear from Tables 4.5 and 4.6, underachievers are found across all the schools sampled with the highest frequency in the predominantly English-Medium school (Schools B, A & C in that order). Over-achievers were found in the highest frequency in School D.

Correlates of Under- and Over-achievers

For the three groups of normal, under- and Over-achievers, an attempt was made to identify correlates in terms of the range of psychological variables examined. Results are presented in Tables 4.7 and 4.8. Minor differences were found across the 3 groups with the exception of school environment and career worries (see Table 4.7). Over-achievers tended to perceive their school, teachers and fellow students more positively and also had more worries related to their future career. As far as evaluation of academic and learning characteristics is concerned (see Table 4.8), teachers tended to evaluate normal achieving students more positively, while in the case of normal and over-achievers, their parents viewed their academic abilities in a more positive manner.

Table 4.5 : School-wise distribution of Under–, Normal and Over-achievers

School	*Under-Achievers*	*Normal Achievers*	*Over Achievers*
A	22	14	10
B	28	14	8
C	20	18	10
D	12	15	16
E	18	4	8
F	16	9	4
Total	116	74	56

Table 4.6 : School-wise incidence of the degree of Under and Over Achievement

School	*Extreme Under-Achievers*	*Moderate Under-Achievers*	*Marginal Under-Achievers*	*Marginal Over-Achievers*	*Moderate Over-Achievers*
A	2	6	14	6	4
B	4	10	14	8	—
C	—	8	12	5	5
D	1	5	6	12	4
E	2	7	9	5	3
F	—	6	10	4	—
Total	9	42	65	40	16

Table 4.7 : Means and SDs of the Psychological Variables for Under-, Normal and Over-achievers

Psychological Variables		*Under-Achievers*	*Normal Achievers*	*Over-Achievers*
School Environment	M	64.25	63.91	65.38
	SD	8.92	10.24	10.59
Academic Motivation	M	45.14	45.66	45.11
	SD	6.64	6.70	6.82
Affect	M	27.74	27.64	27.30
	SD	3.50	3.89	3.47
School Anxiety	M	22.48	22.56	22.82
	SD	5.91	6.50	5.74
Career Worries	M	16.74	15.94	17.80
	SD	4.15	4.15	4.11

Table 4.8 : Means and SDs of Rating of Academic Ability for Under–, Normal and Over-achievers

Rating of Academic Ability		*Under-Achievers*	*Normal Achievers*	*Over-Achievers*
Students Academic Ability	M	15.33	15.82	15.94
	SD	2.17	2.18	2.34
Teachers	M	14.06	16.12	15.86
	SD	3.33	3.42	3.46
Parents	M	15.99	16.52	16.58
	SD	2.42	1.99	2.41
School Anxiety	M	22.48	22.56	22.82
	SD	5.91	6.50	5.74
Career Worries	M	16.74	15.94	17.80
	SD	4.15	4.15	4.11

Similarly a comparison was made of the scores obtained on the psychological measures across the 5 levels of over- and under-achievement. These results are presented in Tables 4.9 and 4.10. The tables show that moderate over-achievers viewed their school more positively, motivation was found to be high in this group, their academic self-concept was positive and their academic abilities were rated highly by parents and teachers. On the other hand, extreme under-achievers also viewed their school positively, academic motivation was on par and the Affect scores slightly higher than the over-achievers' group, and anxiety and career worries were found to be high. However, their academic self-concept was low and both teachers and parents rated their abilities poorly, relative to the over-achievers.

Table 4.9 : Means and SDs of Psychological Variables for 5 levels of Over and Under-Achievers

Psychological Variables		*UA1*	*UA2*	*UA3*	*OA1*	*OA2*
School	M	66.82	64.84	63.53	64.51	67.50
Environment	SD	11.57	10.02	7.83	10.66	10.46
Academic	M	45.22	44.73	45.39	44.81	45.81
Motivation	SD	8.56	6.77	6.35	7.14	6.18
Affect	M	28.28	28.29	27.33	27.13	27.79
	SD	3.95	3.70	3.31	3.36	3.49
School	M	22.33	22.44	22.52	22.18	24.38
Anxiety	SD	4.50	5.89	6.16	5.29	6.62
Career	M	17.00	17.29	16.34	18.15	16.94
Worries	SD	3.94	4.09	4.24	4.21	3.82

Note : For abbreviations (UA1, UA2 etc.) see text.

Table 4.10 : Means and SDs of Rating of Academic Ability for levels of Over- and Under-Achievers

Rating of Academic Ability		*UA1*	*UA2*	*UA3*	*OA1*	*OA2*
Students	M	15.25	15.51	15.23	15.92	16.00
	SD	1.49	2.22	2.24	2.29	2.57
Teachers	M	14.63	13.08	14.54	15.61	16.33
	SD	3.50	3.43	3.19	3.38	3.70
Parents	M	15.50	16.08	16.00	16.39	17.07
	SD	2.20	2.19	2.63	2.50	2.17

Note : For abbreviations (UA1, UA2 etc.) see text.

Factors Related to Achievement and Under-Achievement

To further investigate the factors related to achievement and under-achievement, correlations were computed for the scale factors (factors extracted following factor analysis of the psychological scales) which were treated as dependent measures and outcome measures. The variables included in this level of analysis are presented in Table 4.11.

Table 4.11: Dependent and Outcome Measures

Dependent Measures		
Scale	*Factor*	*Acronym*
School Environment	1. Interesting School	Intsch
	2. Supportive Teachers	Suptch
	3. School Image	Schimg
	4. Fair Teachers	Fatch
	5. Attention to Personal Problems	Att
	6. Peer Support	Pesp
Academic Motivation	1. Irksome	Irk
	2. Study Involvement	Invol
	3. Negative Motivation	Nmot
	4. Striving	Strv
Affect	1. Emotional Control	Emcont
	2. Emotional Reticence	Emret
	3. Empathy	Emp
	4. Oversensitivity	Ovsen
	5. Emotional Recovery	Emrec
School Anxiety	1. School Anxiety	Scanx
Career Worries	1. Career Worries	Carwor

Outcome Measures	
Name	Acronym
1. Total score on SPM	RPMT
2. Half Yearly Exam Percentage	HEXP
3. Half Yearly Exam Arithmetic Percentage	ARTP
4. Previous Year Exam Percentage	PEXP
5. Previous Year Exam Arithmetic Percentage	PATP
6. Academic Abilities Rated by Teacher	ACTT
7. Academic Abilities Rated by Parents	ACPT
8. Academic Abilities Rated by Students	ACSF

The correlation data generated was voluminous and it would not be possible to present all the data here. Therefore, it was resolved to include only those variables for which significant correlations were obtained. This is presented in Table 4.12.

Table 4.12 : Correlations between Dependent and Outcome measures

OUTCOME MEASURES

Dependent Measures	*RPMT*	*HEXP*	*ARTP*	*PEXP*	*PATP*	*ACTT*	*ACPT*	*ACSF*
INTSCH	-.13**	.14*	.05	-.03	.05	.04	.12	.26**
SUPTCH	-.11*	.06	.14	.01	.04	.01	.19*	.28**
SCHIMG	-.07	-.03	.03	-.18*	.16*	.17*	-.00	.21**
ATT	-.11*	-.04	.04	-.03	-.02	-.06	.14*	.02
PESP	-.01	-.06	-.06	-.08	-.14*	-.11	.02	.13*
IRK	.01	.08	.27**	-.00	-.02	.16*	.21**	.38**
INVOL	.18**	.15*	.23**	.19**	.16*	.08	.14*	.03
NMDT	.14*	.18**	.31**	.18**	.13	.15*	.15*	.15*
STRV	.22**	.24**	.22**	.16*	.09	.18*	.06	.14*
EMCONT	.06	-.01	-.05	-.08	-.06	.07	.20**	.28**
EMRET	.07	-.06	.01	.00	-.01	-.10	.05	.19**
EMPT	.09	.10	.07	.20**	.09	.02	-.023	-.11
OVSEN	.26**	.11	.17*	.23**	.17*	.09	.09	-.03
SCANX	-.15*	-.015*	-.15*	-.12	-.06	-.14	-.34**	-.51**
CARWOR	-.24**	-.15*	-.25**	-.22**	-.17*	-.12	-.21**	-.25**

Note : * p < .05 ** p < .01 For full form of acronyms, see Table 4.11

Perusal of these results show that the factors related to the school environment scale (Interesting School, Supportive teachers and Attention to personal problems) correlated negatively with the ability measure (RPMT). Also school anxiety and career worries correlated negatively with the objective indices of performance (HEXP and PEXP) and with parent's and student's evaluation of their academic and learning characteristics (ACPT and ACSF). Positive correlations were found between academic motivation factors, ability, and performance measures, parents, and students' ratings. The Affect scale factors (emotional control and emotional reticence) were significantly correlated only with ACPT and ACSF. Only over sensitivity/reflexivity and to some extent empathy related significantly with the objective indices. Further, it was evident that among the outcome measures, it was the rating of academic abilities (Academic Self-Concept) of students (ACSF) which showed the most consistent relationship with all the scale factors. Accordingly, the correlations between ACSF and the scale factors were computed. In an effort to explore the unique relationships between these variables in each school, a school-wise analysis was done. The results are presented in Table 4.13.

Table 4.13 : Correlation between Dependent Measures & Academic Self Concept

Dependent Measures	Schools					
	A	B	C	D	E	F
INTSCH	.14	.27	.21	.41**	.18	.32*
SUPTCH	.18	.25	-.07	.54**	.44**	.34*
SCHIMG	-.01	.21	.16	.32*	.25`	.23
ATT	.04	.34*	-.07	.06	-.00	-.12
PESP	-.14	.14	.35*	.15	.00	.29
IRK	.30	.37*	.25	.53**	.28	.59**
NMOT	.30	.31*	.28	.29	-.04	.09
STRV	.21	.12	.48**	-.17	.20	.14
EMCONT	.46**	.19	.08	.34*	.46**	.32*
EMRET	.42**	.19	.22	.18	.27	-.02
SCANX	-.53**	-.57**	-.31**	-.42**	-.47**	-.65**
CARWOR	-.44**	-.58**	-.09	.07	-.23	-.08

Note : * p < .05 ** p < .01 For full form of acronyms, See Table 4.1.1

Again, it is clear from these results that across all schools, there was a strong negative relationship between school anxiety and ACSF. For two schools (A and B), a similar trend was observed in the case of Career Worries. The School Environment factors showed a significant positive relationship with ACSF mainly for School D, the academic motivation factors showed a positive relationship mainly in the case of Schools B and C and the Affect scale factors (emotional control and reticence) showed a significant relationship in the case of School A and to a lesser extent for Schools E and F.

To further examine the differences across scale factors for levels of over-, under- and normal achievers, ANOVAs were computed. These results are presented in Table 4.14. Apart from the Affect scale factor, emotional recovery [F=2.84, df (4, 166) p <.05], none of the ratios were significant. To test for differences between groups, the Student–Newman–Keuls procedure (Multiple Range Text) was used. This showed significant differences between two groups of under achievers : Moderate and Marginal.

Table 4.14 : ANOVA results for scale factors and five levels of Over-, and Under-Achievement

Scale Factors	*F*	*Means*				
		UA1	*UA2*	*UA3*	*OA1*	*OA2*
INTSCH	1.51					
SUPTCH	1.90					
SCHIMG	.89					
FATCH	.43					
ATT	.21					
PESP	.33					
IRK	.15					
INVOL	.78					
NMOT	.78					
STRV	.55					
EMCONT	.98					
EMRET	.68					
EMP	.51					
OVSEN	.36					
EMREC	2.84*	2.78	3.36	2.92	3.1	3.5
SCANX	.43					
CAROWR	.59					

Note : * p < .05. For full form of acronyms, see Table 4.10 and text.

Similarly, ANOVAs were computed to test for difference between over-, under- and normal achievers. Results are presented in Table 4.15. With the exception of Career Worries [F = 3.11, df (2, 24) p<.05], none of the ratios were significant. For Career Worries, significant differences were observed between the Normal and Over-achievers groups.

Table 4.15 : ANOVA results for Scale Factors and 3 levels of Achievement

		ACHIEVERS		
Scale Factors	*F*	*Means*		
		Under	*Normal*	*Over*
INTSCH	.58			
SUPTCH	1.90			
SCHIMG	1.31			
FATCH	.22			
ATT	.47			
PESP	.08			
IRK	.21			
INVOL	.05			
NMOT	.05			
STRV	.62			
EMCONT	.92			
EMRET	.06			
EMP	.12			
OVSEN	.79			
EMREC	.84			
SCANX	.06			
CARWOR	3.11*	11.23	10.44	12.13

Note: * $p < .05$, For full form of acronyms, see Table 4.10

Table 4.16 : Parents' Rating of Counsellor Need

School	*Mean*	*SD*	*No. of Parents*
A	31.57	4.40	46
B	32.10	3.88	48
C	33.16	4.47	47
D	32.33	4.39	40
E	33.26	4.02	31
F	32.41	4.60	41
Total	32.41	4.30	253

Note : Range for total scores is 13 –39.

Table 4.17 : Teachers' Rating of Counsellor Need

School	*Mean*	*SD*	*No. of Teachers*
A	36.6	2.06	5
B	34.88	4.95	9
C	36.71	3.77	7
D	34.83	2.41	8
E	30.71	5.06	7
F	32.6	5.35	6
Total	34.37	4.73	42

Note : Range for total scores is 15 – 45

Counsellor Need

Teachers and parents had also completed a Need for School Counsellor Scale. A school-wise analysis was done for the data obtained from parents and teachers. The results are presented in Tables 4.16 and 4.17. Across all schools, parents had high mean scores and a similar trend was observed in the case of teachers, signifying that the need for a school counsellor was imperative. In addition, ratings of teachers and parents for individual items and different counsellor functions were also compared. The results are presented in Table 4.18. Again, parents and teachers uniformly endorsed all counsellor functions as being essential (scale point 2) or very essential (scale point 3). For most scale items, parents gave higher mean ratings. In particular, counsellor functions such as, parent counselling and advising teachers were rated as being somewhat less important by teachers.

Table 4.18 : Parents' and Teacher' Ratings of Counsellor Functions

Item #	*Counsellor Function*	*Parents*		*Teachers*	
		M	*SD*	*M*	*SD*
1	Personal Counselling	2.52	.61	2.40	.59
	" "	-	-	2.45	.59
2	Helping with learning-related problems	2.66	.52	2.46	.91

(Contd.....)

Table 4.18 *(Contd.....)*

Item	*Counsellor Function*	*Parents*		*Teachers*	
		M	*SD*	*M*	*SD*
7	Helping with learning-related problems	2.61	.54	2.45	.50
3	Assessment of Abilities	2.40	.64	2.27	.67
4	" "	2.62	.55	2.48	.55
5	" "	2.52	.60	2.44	.63
6	Career Planning	2.43	.62	2.27	.71
11	" "	2.47	.63	2.24	.71
8	Parent Counselling	2.44	.64	2.24	.69
12	" "	2.21	.74	2.15	.74
13	" "	2.49	.59	2.36	.69
15	" "	-	-	2.32	.52
9	Advising Teachers	2.30	.67	2.0	.74
10	" "	2.47	.59	2.02	.75

Note: Range for Mean Scores is 1–3.

Chapter 5

DISCUSSION

Contemporary researchers are fully aware of the multidimensionality of factors that affect children's achievement outcomes (Honig, 1990). Societal effect, peer effect, teacher influences and the contribution of the child's own behaviours on parents can all shape the ultimate levels of child cognitive and academic competence and personal adjustment.

In light of the above perspective, this discussion will focus on the principal findings and attempt to address those issues, which constituted the major objectives of the study (outlined in the Method chapter). Brief case studies of under- and over-achievers will also be presented.

The primary objective of this study was to ascertain the prevalence of academic underachievement in selected schools of Allahabad. Using an *Index of Underachievement,* which was devised for this study and included composite criteria, this study, found that approximately 47 per cent of the sample studied could be classified as underachievers. Normal achievers comprised 30 per cent of the sample and 23 per cent of the sample had academic achievement exceeding their ability (See Table 4.4)

The incidence of underachievement was comparatively higher in the predominantly English-medium schools (Schools B, A and C) (see Tables 4.5and 4.6). The highest numbers of underachievers were found in School B (N = 28) which is 56 per cent of the school sample. Among the underachievers, 4 were placed in the extreme and 10 and 14 in the moderate and marginal underachieving groups. In School A, 22 underachievers were identified (44 per cent of the school sample) with 2, 6 and 14 students being placed in the extreme, moderate and marginal underachieving groups, respectively. In School C, 20 underachievers were identified (40% of the school sample), with 8 moderate and 12 marginal underachievers. Overachievers (i.e. students whose academic performance exceeded their intellectual abilities) were found across all schools, but mainly in School D where 16 students (32% of the school sample) were classified as overachievers.

These are significant findings as they indicate the severity and magnitude of the problem. Most, earlier studies (e. g. Weiner, 1982) had reported a lower incidence generally in the range of 25 per cent of the student population. Undoubtedly, then the need to understand the factors which contribute to underachievement and the imperatives to develop effective intervention strategies to tackle this problem assume salience.

Our understanding of how the ecology of the classroom and the school as a whole influence children's cognitive, emotional and social development remains underdeveloped at the present time. For the most part, researchers interested in children's education have focused on the impact of schools on intellectual rather than on social-emotional outcomes in children (Eccles, Lord, & Roesner, 1996), and researchers interested in social-emotional development have focused mainly on the socializing influence of the family, peer group and neighbourhood, rather than the school. For decades, evidence has been available that structural and demographic variables, such as, parental education and income level were significantly associated with schooling success. But these socio-economic variables do not account for the complexity of child achievement outcomes. More evidence has become available over the past quarter century, that family process variables and parental expectancies, values, responsivities and tutorial effects are equally if not more dynamically related to children's achievement (Honig, 1990). For this reason, this study sought parents' views about their child's academic abilities and performance and their future hopes and expectations regarding their child. Apart from parents, the school also has a critical if not vital role to play in shaping achievement. The school as a social institution reflects the culture of which it is a part and transmits to the young an ethos and world view as well as specific skills and knowledge (Minuchin & Shapiro, 1983). Psychologists look at the school as an environment for individual development. Children spend years in school as members of a small society in which there are tasks be done, people to relate to and rules that define the possibilities of behaviour. Such experiences affect the sense of self, the belief in one's competence and relationship to other people. It would be appropriate at this point to examine the scores of the School Environment scale which consisted of the following factors: interesting school, supportive teachers, school image, fair teachers, attention to personal problems, peer support. At least 4 of these factors showed significant differences across the schools studied. Apart from students of School D, most students rated their schools as being dull and boring, with students of Schools B and C obtaining the lowest scores on the interesting school factor.

Across schools, teachers were perceived as being less supportive. Here, as well, differences were observed across schools. Students of Schools D and A found their teachers to be moderately supportive, while students of Schools F, B and C found their teachers to be less supportive. Items related to teachers being fair and impartial in evaluation and disciplinary matters generally received low to moderate ratings. Again school differences were observed. School F students perceived their teachers as being fair and unbiased while students of Schools C and B felt their teachers were partial in evaluation and inconsistent and capricious in implementing disciplinary practice.

Across schools, the school image was generally seen as being positive. Children's perceptions of the classroom or school environment are stronger predictors of their adjustment than are more "objective" indicators of the environment such as observers' ratings (Ryan & Grolnick, 1986; Weinstein, 1989). School effects on achievement and other achievement-related behaviours are mediated through children's perceptions of the environment (Eccles, *et al.*, 1998). Again School D students had more positive views and students of other schools (notably School F) were somewhat less positive. It is pertinent to highlight the fact that the highest incidence of underachievement was found in Schools B and C and consistently students of these schools found their school and teachers to be less facilitative of their personal and academic growth. As pointed out by Ma (www.ctd.northwestern.edu) when students underachieve they feel badly about themselves. One of the ways that they cope with these negative self-perceptions is by minimizing the importance of school.

Similarly, the highest incidence of over achievement was found in School D where the school and teachers were seen more positively and as being more supportive. An important constituent of the school system is the teacher. It has often been assumed that the teacher has an equivalent impact on all children in the class. Any description of classroom life, however, throws into relief the particularity of the teacher's interaction with different children. Quality teacher-student relationships positively affect students' motivation to learn and their "bonding" with the institution of school. (Goodenow, 1993; Midgley, Feldlaufer, & Eccles, 1989b; Moos, 1979; Roeser, Midgley, & Urdan, 1996). Conversely, a lack of supportive teacher relationships can fuel students' alienation from school (Fine, 1991). This study, accordingly examined teachers' views regarding their students' academic and learning characteristics. The consequent impact of their views was also examined while preparing a descriptive profile of under-, normal and over- achievers. These profiles will be briefly discussed.

The descriptive profiles of the three groups which emerged following interpretation of the results presented in Tables 4.7 and 4.8 are as follows: on the psychological variables, underachievers as a group (combining the three levels of extreme, moderate and marginal underachievers) perceived their school environment in a moderately positive manner, their academic motivation was high, on the Affect scale they obtained the highest scores and their school anxiety and career-related worries were found to be in the low-moderate range. However, as far as ratings for academic abilities were concerned, their own academic self-concept was found to be the lowest while parents and teachers rated them poorly in comparison with the normal and overachiever's groups.

The descriptive profiles of the other two groups of normal and over-achievers on the psychological variables were somewhat similar. This is borne out by the fact that ANOVAS that were computed to examine differences across scale factors were not significant with the exception of career-worries (see Table 4.15). Here it was found that the overachievers had significantly higher scores on the Career Worries scale.

Previous studies have posited that lack of a specific career goal is indicative of low vocational maturity. Students showing career indecision were found to have low academic motivation and work involvement. This is because making wise career decisions is one of the critical school problems of adolescence (Phillips, 1983). Specifically, for this study, it is possible to make the inference that high scores on Career Worries is indicative of a greater concern for formulating concrete career goals and this in turn is facilitative of academic achievement.

When differences were examined across the five levels of over- and underachievement, Emotional Recovery (Affect scale) was found to be highest in the Moderate overachievers' group, and significant differences were observed between the Moderate and Marginal underachiever groups.

Emotional recovery in this study was conceptualised as a basic emotional skill, which includes the capacity to soothe oneself, to shake off anxiety, gloom and irritability (Goleman, 1995). People who are poor in this ability are battling feelings of distress while those who excel in it can bounce back more quickly from life's setbacks and upsets. A sense of self-mastery, of being able to recover from emotional storms has long been praised as a virtue. The goal is balance, not emotional suppression. It has also been found that extremes-emotions that wax too intensely or to long can undermine the individual's stability.

As pointed out by Goleman (1995), the design of the brain means that we very often have no control ***when*** we are swept by emotion, nor over ***what*** emotion it will be. But we can have some say in ***how long*** an emotion will last (p. 64). The implications are clear: intense emotions, which linger past an appropriate point, can lead to distressing outcomes. As far as adjustment to concerned, it seems that a contribution to academic success (in particular, achievement exceeding one's cognitive abilities) is the ability to feel appropriate emotions and to quickly recover after an emotional event.

The next set of variables, which were examined, was related to students', teachers' and parents' ratings of academic and learning characteristics. Studies have shown that there are certain cognitive processes which translate academic problems into subsequent emotional distress. One such process involve the manner in which students cognitively appraise their academic difficulties, with specific kinds of attributions for difficulty leading directly to feelings of internalized or externalized distress (Ames & Archer, 1988; Weiner, 1994). Students who do poorly in school and who attribute such difficulties to a fixed sense of personal incompetence generate feelings of shame, self-doubt, low esteem and alienation from learning. Students' appraisal of academic difficulty can impact on their developing self-perceptions of academic competence, academic value, and beliefs about the relative supportedness of others in learning situations. Competence beliefs, values, and feelings of support are associated with feelings of esteem, interest and belonging, whereas feelings of incompetence, low value and low support are associated with feelings of shame and doubt, disinterest and boredom and isolation or victimization (Ames, 1992, Eccles *et al*., 1998; Roeser, Eccles, & Strobel, 1998).

Here, over-achievers rated their own abilities more positively while for normal achievers, teachers and parents rated their academic abilities most positively. These findings showcase the fact that the critical variables, which differentiate between these three groups (i. e. Over, Normal, and Under-achievers) is how they perceive their own academic qualities and abilities and how they are rated by their parents and teachers. In the case of Normal Achievers, parents and teachers credit them with sterling academic qualities and these students then live up to their parents' and teachers' expectations. It also paves the way for a more positive rating of their own abilities.

As far as over-achievers are concerned, they rate their own academic abilities more positively and so do their parents. As a consequence they tend to out do themselves, with their performance outstripping their abilities. In some school children there is a pattern of co-occurring academic success and emotional well-being (Roeser & Eccles, 2000). In this case, positive attributions for success (e.g., effort and hard work) contribute to these students' sense that they are competent and school is valuable. These beliefs in turn lead to feelings of pride, high self-esteem, and enjoyment of learning (Deci & Ryan, 1985; Weiner, 1986). Feelings of psychological well-being in turn activate positive motivational beliefs (e.g., competence beliefs, values) and serve to focus such students' attention on mood-congruent, positive aspects of the school environment such as moments of success, the intrinsically motivating qualities of tasks, and supports for learning. These motivational beliefs, in concert with attention to supportive contextual factors and experiences, predict subsequent academic success (Eccles, 1983; Pintrinch & De Groot, 1990).

In addition, these students show a preference for moderately challenging tasks, a redoubling of effort following difficulty, participation in classroom activities, free-time choice of academic activities and high achievement. In terms of qualitative processes, such students pursue goals associated with academic mastery and self-improvement, attribute successes to hard work and cope with the inevitable setbacks that occur during learning by redoubling their efforts and seeking help. In general, students who manifest the intrinsic-mastery organizational pattern of behaviour can be characterised as somewhat optimistic, reflective, flexible, and intrinsically self-regulated (Ames, 1992; Deci & Ryan, 1985; Dweck & Legget, 1988; Nicholls, 1984).

For the underachievers group unfortunately, their teachers have very low expectations from them. Their parents as well rate their academic abilities negatively (but not as negatively as do teachers) and this negative assessment impacts on their academic self-concept so that they tend to perceive themselves less positively.

When a detailed analysis was done across the five levels of under- and over-achievement, similar trends were observed (see Table 4.10). As far as student ratings were concerned the moderate and marginal over-achievement groups tended to perceive their academic qualities more positively then the underachievement groups. Recent studies have shown that underachieving students are impulsive and inaccurate in their self-judgments regarding prior knowledge of a topic to be learned and in judging their own capacities, given specific task demands (Borkowski & Thorpe, 1994). Conversely, academically successful students demonstrated a greater degree of self-regulation and willingness to persist on tasks than their less-successful peers (Wibrowski, 1992).

Teachers rated moderate underachievers very negatively (M = 13.08), while over-achievers, in particular the moderate over-achievers were seen in a more positive light (M = 19.33). As far as moderate over-achievers were concerned, their parents viewed their academic abilities in a most positive manner (M = 17.07) while the extreme underachievers received the lowest ratings (M = 15.50). But in general, across all groups, parents were more sympathetically inclined and generally saw there offsprings' abilities in a more positive light. It is clear that the crucial variable was the teachers' assessments and evaluations that differentiated between the groups.

Correlational data (Tables 4.12 and 4.13) also needs to be considered here. Among the outcome measures, academic self-concept was most consistently related to all the scale factors. Across all schools, school anxiety showed a strong negative relationship with Academic self-concept. Further for two schools (Schools A and B), Career Worries was negatively correlated with student perception of their academic qualities. Relevant studies include those of Humachek (1971; cf. A.K. Gupta & S.K. Sharma, 1987) who found that the way a student views himself/herself accounts for academic success. It was found that aspirations and the drive to succeed are good predictors of achievement. S. Sharma (1975) further substantiated the finding that high anxiety interferes with academic performance.

Several studies have focused on teachers' expectations of children's academic performance and the fact that teachers have different expectations for different children. The most widely known study is that of Rosenthal and Jacobson's ***Pygmalion in the classroom*** (1968). The findings suggested a self-fulfilling prophecy and showed that what teachers expect from children will influence how they treat them and that this will affect how the children actually perform.

More recent studies have suggested that because teachers expect certain kind of behaviour from high achievers and different behaviour from low achievers they treat them differently and thereby sustain these patterns (Cooper, 1979; Good, 1980). High achievers are given more opportunities to participate in class and more time to respond. They receive more praise and less criticism than low achievers. Low achievers are expected not to know and not to participate and are given less opportunity for doing so. Cooper's hypothesis is that the teacher initiates more interactions with successful students because their behaviour is more predictable. He also posits that students for whom the teacher has high expectations are criticised when the teacher thinks they have not tried and praised when they do try. On the other hand, students, for whom the teacher has low expectations are both praised and criticised for reasons irrelevant to their effort. These findings clearly demonstrate the impact of teachers' expectations on the academic performance of students.

Studies in India (review by B. Kaur, Menon & Konantambigi, 2001) have recognized that schools and families are the primary contexts for socialization and learning and have investigated the linkages between home and school (Kaur, 1994). It was found that teachers seldom provided academic support to those children who were most likely to need it. Teachers perceived them to lack in ability and effort for learning, and belong to homes which did not value education. The mutual mistrust between parents and teachers were likely to lead to poor learning. The implications are clear: teachers need to be aware and sensitive as to how their evaluations of students impact on their expectations from students and eventually influence the actual performance of their students.

Parental expectations also assume great significance, as expectancy formation is a critical determinant of goal directed activity. That is, which achievement activities children pursue—as well as the intensity, duration and quality of that pursuit is related to their confidence that they can realise their goals. A number of studies have examined the general correlates and consequences of high and low expectancies. Parental practices associated with high grades of children appear similar to those practices associated with potentially debilitating motivational patterns. Specifically, the former are found to be a high degree of parental dominance, pressure, evaluation and criticism (Miller, 1970; Teichmann, Gollnitz & Gohler, 1975). Similarly, the latter, debilitating motivational patterns are often found to be related to unreasonable parental expectations for the child, overly direct intrusive help (versus general facilitating assistance); criticism for errors (versus praise for progress) and the use of normative standards for judgement (Baumrind, 1971, 1973; Hermans, Ter-Laak & Maes, 1972).

As far as gender differences in expectancy are concerned many intriguing findings have been reported. Crandall (1969) reports a number of studies in which girls of different ages generated lower expectancies than boys, even on tasks on which they outperformed boys. Moreover, it was the brightest girls who were underestimated the most. In a more recent study, Stipek and Hoffman (1980) found that the highest-achieving girls actually had lower expectancies of success than the average or low-achieving girls. Parental expectations also seem to favour boys over girls. Studies by Williams (1972) found that fathers emphasised the affective aspects of achievement situations for daughters and parents formed high educational aspirations more readily for males than for females. In this study, it was found that teachers rated the academic abilities of girls *vis-à-vis* those of boys, more positively than boys (see Table 4.2). In interpreting these results we will again take recourse to expectancy theory which states that expectancies are related to persistence, performance and academic achievement. It stands to reason following expectancy theory that low or negative evaluations and the consequent expectancies generated by them can contribute to academic underachievement. In particular, the role of teachers is significant in this process. Research evidence will now be used to both substantiate and moderate this viewpoint.

Research on teacher-student interactions in the classroom have failed to revel any consistent, "facilitating" interaction style that teachers display toward high versus low achievers (Brophy & Good, 1974; Brophy,1979). Dweck and Elliott (1983) postulate that there may be many motivational routes to high or low achievement outcomes. Specifically, they suggest that learning goals when the child holds a high value for the skills to be learned or has a high interest in the tasks to be performed in school may foster high goals. High grades may also be fostered by both of the performance goals when there is high confidence in attaining these goals and when the child places high value on adults' judgements. Indeed, according to Dweck and Elliott (1983) this combination may yield an excessively high effort pattern and seems to be the most plausible explanation for the over achievement in schools such as School D.

Low grades as well can be associated with either learning or performance goals, as for example, when children who tend to have learning goals, find low value or interest in school activities or when children who tend to have performance goals place low value on the teacher's evaluation (e.g. versus those of peers) or have low expectancies of obtaining positive evaluations and avoiding negative ones which may be the case in schools such as B and C.

The teacher's instructional interactional style with particular children is also a significant determinant. Teachers who favour incremental theories of intelligence and learning goals for children (as opposed to those with entity views and performance goals) would be predicted to act more as resources *versus* judges, to focus more on process *versus* outcome, to react to errors as natural and useful *versus* as failures, to stress effort and personal standards versus ability and normative standards, to stimulate achievement through intrinsic *versus* extensive means.

Further, as pointed out by Dweck and Elliott (1983) children are not simply victims or beneficiaries of adults' practices; they are often accomplices and sometimes even instigators. That is children who act in particular ways may "pull" certain behaviour from adults that, in turn, may promote and perpetuate certain motivational patterns.

Partial support for some of the theoretical contentions stated above may be found in the result obtained in this study. If we consider the case of School D as the school with the highest number of overachievers and School B as the school with the highest number of underachievers and compare these schools on the psychological parameters studied it is clear that School D students viewed their school most positively and found their teachers to be supportive and impartial. Students of School B on the other hand found school to be the least interesting, teachers less supportive and more partial and inconsistent in evaluation and disciplinary matters.

Again, if we consider the scale factors of the Academic Motivation scale, two factors "Irksome" and "Study Involvement" showed significant differences across schools. Generally speaking students from all schools found studies to be irksome with the greatest burden being perceived by students of Schools F and E and the least burden by students of School C, study involvement was also found to be low to moderate across schools. The greatest involvement was found in Schools A, E and B students and the lowest involvement in School F students. For the Affect scale, the over sensitivity factor showed significant differences across schools. Generally scores were low across schools with students of Schools A, B and C (schools with the highest number of underachievers) getting higher scores and School D and F students (School D had the highest number of overachievers) obtaining low scores. It seems that over sensitivity in emotional matters can interfere to some extent with academic pursuits.

Finally, this discussion will focus on the need for the services of school psychologists and counsellors. One of the unequivocal findings of this study was that across all schools and across parents and teachers groups the need for a school counsellor received unanimous endorsement. In fact both groups of respondents felt that school counsellors would have a significant role to play in enhancing and promoting the quality of education (see Tables 4.16-4.18).

It is important therefore to define and clarify the role and functions of the school psychologist/counsellor keeping in mind the specifics of the local context in which they would be required to function (Thapa, 1998). School psychologists as pointed out by Anastasi (1979) work not only in a school but ***through*** it. They serve as consultants to educational personnel and they utilise the school environment as a microcosm of medium. It is equally relevant to note that schools as a microcosm of society need to accept more and more responsibility for childhood adolescent manifestations of society's problems. This is because schools as a part of society share in the responsibility of responding to these problems. Thus as pointed out by Baker (1996) school counsellors need to provide proactive programmes that meet and enhance psychological growth in children.

One important function of school psychologists would be to provide counselling for personal problems. This would include providing psychological help for the entire range of learning, behavioural and emotional problems faced by students in schools. A second function would relate to career planning and assisting students in acquiring and processing information. For example, students could be assisted in using informational resources and in formulating occupational preferences. Assessment is another area in which school counsellors can contribute by using a wide range of strategies to gather information about students. Psychological assessment can be used for classifying students, as an important educational and vocational guidance tool and for predicting academic and occupational success. In the consultation role, school psychologists can work with parents and teachers to facilitate personality development, affective balance and the overall growth and development of their children/students.

Bemoaning the lack of school psychologists in India in general and in Allahabad, in particular, Williams (1997) a school psychologist herself, with the keen perception of the outsider, showcased the problems she observed in Allahabad schools. These included large numbers of students in classes, an overemphasis on rote learning, greater pressures for achievement and the fact that only certain professions (Civil Services, engineering and medical professions) are viewed as being prestigious. She also found schools to be less child-centred. These according to her were basic and sufficient reasons to induct school psychologists into the school system.

The next section will include brief case studies of under- and over-achievers.

Chapter 6

CASE-STUDIES

The case-study approach facilitates a more comprehensive and personalised study of individual students. For this purpose, students were randomly selected from two groups: Extreme underachievers (N = 9) and Moderate over-achievers (N = 16). The first two case studies focus on an under-achiever and over-achiever both from the same school, School A. This was done to examine critical differences between under-and over-achievers who were exposed to the same school environment and possibly similar instructional styles and a uniform educational ethos and ambience. The next two case studies focus on an under-achiever from School E and an over-achiever from School D where again presumably there is greater concordance in educational and instructional practices. Additional case studies are included following the same strategy, in that a detailed case study of an extreme underachiever is paired with that of a moderate overachiever from the same or similar school. All case studies have been formulated on the basis of the data collected for the study from students, parents and teachers.

Case Study I

GS I (only initials are being used to maintain anonymity) is a student of class IX of School A (ID # 003). His SPM score was a perfect 60, which is indicative of superior intelligence. On the contrary his half-yearly marks totalled 46 per cent, the Arithmetic percentage was 33 per cent, previous examination percentage was 41 per cent, and previous Arithmetic percentage was 40 per cent. The Index of underachievement was computed using SPM scores (Grade 1) and previous Examination percentage (Level 5). The obvious discrepancy between ability and performance resulted in GS I being placed in the *Extreme Underachievement* group.

On the School Environment scale, he found school to be less interesting, teachers were seen as being less supportive and biased and partial in their interactions with students. There was obvious pride in the school but its disciplinary practices were perceived as being harsh and punitive and inconsistently implemented. The peer group was seen as being less supportive and helpful. Regarding those aspects of the school, which require change, he felt that teachers were partial and gave less emphasis to sports and did not complete their syllabus.

Academic motivation was generally high. For instance, the irksome aspect of studies was less emphasized by him, he was involved and committed and aspired to do well in studies. However, negative incentives led to a decrease in the effort and interest invested in specific subjects.

On the Affect scale, emotional control was found to be adequate and less impulsivity in behaviour was found. However, he was also found to be reticent in emotional matters and was unable to express feelings and emotions in an open manner. GS I was sensitive and empathic towards the feelings of others, though at times he was found to be over sensitive. Emotional recovery was found to be impaired and he reported that emotions often persisted and he was often engulfed by emotions and he was unable to respond to the practical demands of the situation. Regarding the reporting of sad events, he recounted the recent death of his uncle. His reaction was muted and restrained; he reported feelings of disbelief and sadness, but showed emotional reticence. Significantly, no happy events or reactions were reported.

As far as school anxiety is concerned he was apprehensive and fearful at the prospect of being ridiculed in front of others. Career worries were at the lower end of the scale but he did feel that his present studies would help in later career placement.

As far as academic self-concept was concerned GS I described himself as being planful, confident, superior to others and weak in

Math. His own ratings totalled 9 whereas his parent's ratings were higher. They felt he was lazy, less bright, less successful and weak in Math. On the plus side they felt comprehension and memory were good. His Math teacher rated him poorly on all academic abilities but conceded that he was confident. Both parents and teachers felt he had low ability and accordingly rated performance in exams as being poor.

In summary, for GS I the school environment was less facilitative, teachers were seen as being less supportive and more biased and the irksome and negative aspects of academic were dominant. In emotional matters, he tended to be reticent, at the same way time he was often engulfed by emotions, which tended to persist and interfered with his studies. While he viewed his academic abilities and learning characteristics more positively, his parents to a lesser degree and teachers to a considerable degree viewed him as a loser, which propensity, his lowered academic output tended to confirm.

Case Study II

SS is also a student of class IX of School A (ID # 019). On the SPM, she obtained a score of 44 (Grade III, Intellectually average) and her previous academic record was as follows: Half-yearly exam percentage 74 per cent, with 84 per cent in Arithmetic previous year's annual exam percentage 78 per cent (Level 1) with 70 per cent in Arithmetic. SS with Level 1 marks and Grade III ability was placed in the *moderate overachiever's* group.

She viewed school as being very interesting, teachers as being emotionally supportive, appreciative and facilitative, and had a sense of pride and belongingness in the school. In her school experiences she found teachers to be fair and consistent in their implementation of discipline-related rules and in their evaluation. However, this positive picture was marred by the fact that teachers were less attentive to personal problems and also directed less-efforts towards academically poor students. The peer group was also seen as being less supportive. For school in general, she was appreciative of infrastructural facilities (library, competitions held) and teacher behaviour. She also observed that sports facilities and science laboratories were far from adequate and some students vitiated the school environment.

SS's academic motivation was found to be very high. For instance, she viewed academic pursuits in a positive manner and did not perceive them as a burden or as being irksome. Similarly her involvement in studies was great, she was less influenced by negative incentives and had high educational aspirations.

Her emotional balance was adequate. However, she admitted to being easily provoked to anger and rage, she retaliated in equal measure to offensive remarks made by others, sometimes in haste without considering the matter fully and was often envious of the success of others. In other words, she tended to be emotionally impulsive and less controlled and often gave vent to her feelings. However, somewhat paradoxically, she also reported that she was unable to share her innermost thoughts and feelings with others, was after troubled by what others thought about her and brooded over matters. In other words, while she could express negative feelings like anger and resentment in a more assertive manner, a balance was being maintained in the sense that she was reticent and reserved in sharing certain emotions with others. At the same time, she reported being sensitive and empathic to others, but was not over sensitive, though some degree of reflexivity was acknowledged. Again, as far as emotional recovery was concerned, she brooded over matters but could still respond to the functional demands of the situation.

The happy event reported dealt with what she perceived to be an achievement in the academic sphere, in that while previously, she could not obtain a rank, she stood fifth in class. This indicates that even a modest achievement was seen in a positive light and spurred her to greater interest and involvement in studies. The sad event related to her entire family turning against her on some matter (details not given). Though, she felt "tense and disturbed" and it affected her work, she made efforts to clarify the misunderstanding.

A moderate degree of school anxiety was reported. She was

somewhat apprehensive before exams, feared ridicule and humiliation in school and felt that parents expected results exceeding her ability. In career worries, as well, there was concern and worry about not being able to get the aspired for job, but in general, she felt no pressure from her parents and she felt that her present studies would enhance here job prospects.

SS's academic self-concept was generally positive, but she also had a realistic perception of her own abilities and was well aware of her own limitations. She described herself as being hard working, studious, planful, bright, successful and confident. At the same time, she felt that she was not very sharp in understanding, her memory was poor, she felt, inferior to others and was poor in Math. However, significantly, she mentioned an additional characteristic. She was persistent in her efforts. She also rated her own ability as being less than others and her performance as being better than others. Her parents, on the other hand, viewed her academic abilities in a consistently positive manner. They rated her academic abilities and class performance as being superior. The rating of the teacher showed similar positive trends.

In short, SS viewed school and teachers positively and had high educational aspirations. In the emotional sphere she was able to express anger and resentment in an appropriate, assertive manner but maintained a balance by being reserved and hesitant in sharing personal experiences with others. While she viewed her academic abilities more realistically, both her parents and teachers rated her abilities more positively and her performance according was much better than expected.

Case Study III

MK (ID # 236) is a student of class XI of School E. His SPM scores were 57 (Grade I, Intellectually superior) and his obtained marks were 12 per cent in the half-yearly exams and his previous exam percentage was 51 per cent (Level 4) with 48 per cent in Math. This obvious discrepancy resulted in his being placed in thc *Extreme Underachiever's* group.

While he generally found school to be interesting, he felt that teachers were not supportive and actively discouraged probing questions and did not provide space for an open expression of student viewpoints. Further, teachers failed to infuse confidence in students. Also teachers were seen as being harsh, critical and partial. To add to this uniformly, negative assessment of teachers they were also found to be indifferent towards students' academic and personal problems. In general, school image was found to be positive and the peer group supportive in school, he was appreciative of the infrastructural facilities (good classrooms) and good instructional style of teachers. He deplored the insistence of teachers on coaching and would like to bring about changes in the administration of the school.

In general, academic motivation was found to be high. MK did not view studies as being irksome, his involvement was great and he aspired to do well. However, in his case negative incentives (poor marks) led to feelings of discouragement.

On the Affect scale, emotional control was adequate. However, he was neither passive nor muted in his expression of emotions and retaliated when others behaved in an offensive manner. However, he was very reticent and was unable to share experiences and disclose feelings to others. He was sensitive towards others (empathic) but also tended to be oversensitive. Often he felt overwhelmed and engulfed by his emotional reactions. The happy event reported pertained to passing his high school exams and being rewarded with a computer, which strengthened his resolve to work hard. The sad event dealt with the serious illness of his nephew, where he felt sadness and resolved to become a doctor in order to help those in distress.

On the School Anxiety scale he was found to be fearful and apprehensive at the possibility of being ridiculed and humiliated in front of others and also felt that his parents were putting pressure on him to achieve results exceeding his ability. On the Career Worries scale, he felt he faced an uncertain future mainly because information and guidance related to careers was unavailable.

His academic self-concept was generally poor. He felt he was not bright or successful, he was slow in comprehension, nervous, inferior to others and poor in Math. On the positive side, he felt he was studious, hardworking and planful and good in Biology. He also rated his own ability and performance as being better than others. There was a close correspondence between his ratings and those of his parents, who described his academic abilities, using the more negative adjectives. Surprisingly, his teacher viewed him less negatively than did his parents, but they still viewed him mainly in a negative light.

In short, MK viewed his school teachers as being unsupportive and non-facilitative of academic pursuits. He was motivated to do well but received no encouragement. Emotionally, he was reticent but also felt engulfed by his emotions. Both self and parental ratings of academic abilities were negative while his teacher viewed him less negatively.

Case Study IV

PA, a student of class IX of School D (ID # 162) obtained on SPM score of 27 (Grade IV). This score according to the SPM manual is indicative of below average intellectual functioning. In the half yearly exams her total per cent was 55, with the Arithmetic percentage being 34 per cent. In the previous years exams her percentage was 70 (Level 2) and the Arithmetic percentage was 67 per cent. Thus PA was placed in the *Moderate Overachiever's* group.

Generally, PA viewed her school and academic activities very positively. She felt teachers were supportive and facilitative and provided reinforcement for learning. She felt an acute sense of pride in her school and perceived her teachers as being fair and impartial in evaluation, personal relationship and disciplinary matters. She also felt that teachers were aware of and sensitive to the personal and academic problems of students. The peer-group was also seen as being supportive.

On the Academic Motivation scale, as well PA obtained high scores. She did not perceive studies to be a burden, she had an intrinsic involvement in studies, was less affected by negative incentives and always aspired to be do well.

On the Affect scale, emotional control was found to good and she rarely over-reacted in emotion-provoking situations. She was less reticent in emotional matters and could easily share emotional experiences with others. She was fully empathic and sensitive towards the feelings of others, at times over sensitive as well. However, emotional recovery was found to be good. The happy event reported related to academic success, in particular when her achievement was commensurate with effort. Similarly, the sad event again dealt with her doing less well (coming third when she expected to get the second position in class) and feelings of regret and sorrow.

School anxiety was low to moderate. While she feared examinations and ridicule in class, there was no fear of teachers or parental pressures. Similarly, on the Career Worries scale while she bemoaned the lack of career guidance and literature, there were no parental pressures to pursue a career of their choice and there was some concern and anxiety about future career prospects and opportunities.

PA's view of her own academic abilities, was somewhat in line with her ability score on SPM. For instance, she described herself as being less clever and bright, less successful in studies, nervous, inferior and having a poor memory. She also was aware of her the academic strengths: hard working, studious, planful, quick in comprehension and good in Math. Her parents also had a balanced view of her abilities: they felt she was hardworking and studious but also found her to be slow, nervous and poor in Math. Her teachers also concurred: they described her as studious and hardworking, bright and sharp and felt (as did her parents) that she viewed herself as being superior. They were well aware of her weaknesses: nervous and weak in Math. Significantly, teachers felt she had greater ability *vis-à-vis* other students, her parents felt she had poor ability and she herself, felt her ability was average.

In short, PA viewed her school (including teachers very positively, she was motivated to succeed and emotional control was found to be good. Both school anxiety and career worries were moderate and there were no parental pressures operating on her.

She had a realistic, often accurate view of her own academic strengths and weakness, often similar to the views expressed by her parents and teacher.

Case Study V

GS III is a student of Class IX of School A (ID # 003). He scored a perfect 60 (Grade I, Intellectually Superior) on SPM. However, he obtained 46 per cent in his half-yearly exams with 33 per cent in Arithmetic and his previous Annual examination percentage was 41 (Level 5). This extreme discrepancy between ability and performance resulted in his being placed in the *Extreme Underachiever's* group.

He did not find school very interesting. The teachers were not seen as supportive though they were reported to know each student closely. Teachers were also perceived to be negligent and unaware of the problems of students, harsh in their implementation of disciplinary measures, unfair and infusing little confidence in students. He had a sense of pride in school. GS III did not find the peer group supportive. He observed that some teachers in his school were helpful but sports facilities needed to be upgraded, no extra classes should be take in holidays and the course should be completed in time.

GS III's academic motivation was found to be high. He did not find studies to be irksome or burdensome, there was intrinsic involvement in studies and he was not discouraged by negative incentives and had high educational aspirations.

On the Affect scale, emotional balance was found to be adequate. He admitted that he did not retaliate in equal measure to the insulting remarks of others and was sometimes hasty in his reactions. He was somewhat reticent in sharing his innermost thoughts and feelings with others. He was sensitive and empathic to the distress of others but was neither oversensitive nor reflexive. His emotional recovery was good though he reported a tendency to brood over matters. He observed that his behaviour was guided by the practical demands of the situation. Significantly he had no happy event to report. As far as the sad event was concerned it related to the recent death of his maternal uncle. He reported a sense of unreality following this tragedy and had become withdrawn and sad.

His School Anxiety was moderate and he was especially afraid of being humiliated and ridiculed in class in front of others. He was low on Career Worries though he believed that his present studies would not enhance his career prospects.

GS III had a low academic self-concept. He felt he was planful, quick in comprehension, confident, superior to others, moderately successful and somewhat studious. He reported that he was weak in Math. He rated his abilities as being better than others and his performance as being on par with others. His parents on the other hand, felt he had average ability and that his performance was better than others. Not surprisingly, his teacher described him in predominantly negative terms, assessing his ability and performance as being worse than that of others and his performance not matching with his ability.

In summary, GS III did not find school interesting nor his teachers supportive. He had high educational aspirations and was intrinsically motivated. His emotional balance was good. While he reacted to the insults of others, he was also emotionally reticent. He was moderate and low on school anxiety and career worries respectively. He had a poor academic self-concept. He rated his ability as being better than others while his performance was average. His parents rated his ability as average and felt that his performance was better than others. His teacher had a very negative perception of his academic abilities and performance though he observed that GS III was capable of doing better.

Case Study VI

MS is a student of Class IX of School A (ID # 022). He obtained a score of 47 on SPM (Grade III, Intellectually Average). His previous academic record showed that he obtained 71 per cent in the half-yearly exams with 81 per cent in Math and 77.6 per cent (Level 1) in the preceding Annual examination with 80.5 per cent in Math. With his Level 1 academic performance and Grade II ability, MS was placed in the *Moderate Overachiever* group.

He found school to be very interesting and teachers were seen as supportive. Teachers encouraged freedom of expression in students, were unbiased and fair in their implementation of disciplinary rules and in evaluation. They also paid more attention to weak students. They were, however, perceived to be critical and indifferent toward the personal problems of students. There was obvious pride in the school. The peer group was seen as being supportive. MS was appreciative of the school's discipline (even while finding it very strict) as well as the systematic method of instruction, but he found the school expensive and lacking in computer and sports facilities.

MS obtained high scores on the Academic Motivation scale. He did not find his studies irksome and showed intrinsic involvement in them. Negative incentives spurred him on to greater efforts. He had a high aspiration level.

His emotional balance was found to be adequate though he did retaliate in equal measure when insulted by others. He could share his emotional experiences with others to some extent and was not overly influenced by what others thought of him. He was moderately sensitive toward others and not oversensitive, but he was also somewhat reflexive in his reactions. Emotional recovery was good. There was no tendency to brood. The happy event reported was related to his obtaining 80 per cent in his exams. His reaction to this was overconfidence as a result of which he did not fare too well in his next exam. The sad event pertained to the death of his grandfather. This event evoked a sense of sadness and unhappiness in him and made him more sensitive and attuned to the distress of others.

A moderate degree of school anxiety was reported. He was fearful of his teachers and of the possibility of being embarrassed in front of others and he was apprehensive and nervous about his grades. The pressure of parental expectation was also operating in his case. On the Career Worries scale he felt that he faced an uncertain future, but his present studies would in someway enhance his future prospects. The paucity of career-related information was acutely felt.

MS had a positive academic self-concept. He felt he was successful, quick in comprehension, had a good memory, was superior to others and good in Math. On the negative side, he admitted to feelings of nervousness. He rated both his ability and performance as being average. His parents described him in similar terms, but rated his ability and performance as being better than others and also that his ability was superior to his performance. His parents also used positive attributes to describe MS and viewed both his ability and performance as being far superior to others. The teacher, however, made a more realistic assessment of his ability and rated his performances as exceeding his ability.

In summary, MS had a positive image of his school and teachers and had high educational aspirations. He was balanced in his emotional behaviour, moderate in his emotional expression but could express negative emotions in an appropriate manner. He evaluated both his ability and performance as being average while both his parents and teachers saw him in a more positive light.

Case Study VII

MS II is a student of Class XI of School E (ID # 035). His SPM score was 50 (Grade II, Definitely above the average in intellectual capacity). He obtained 1 per cent in the half-yearly exam (Arithmetic per cent not available) and 49 per cent (Level 5) in the previous annual exam with 41 per cent in Arithmetic. This obvious discrepancy of Grade II ability and Level 5 performance resulted in MS being place in the *Extreme Underachiever's* group.

On the School Environment scale, he found school to be uninteresting and teachers were seen as unsupportive. He had a negative image of his school and he felt his teachers were harsh, inconsistent and punitive in their evaluation and in the implementation of disciplinary rules. Teachers were also perceived as being somewhat partial and unappreciative of students' efforts.

However, he did concede that teachers were uncritical but were not entirely indifferent to the problems of students. Peer support was seen as being abysmal. He lauded the efforts of his Principal and Chemistry teacher. At the same time, his main grouse was that the Principal was inaccessible to students, teaching was carried out in a non-serious manner and disciplinary practices were harsh and punitive.

MS was low on academic motivation. He found studies to be tedious and boring. He made efforts to sustain interest in academic pursuits. He was affected by negative incentives but aspired to do well in class.

On the Affect scale he was found to have less emotional control in that he was easily provoked to rage, was not easily pacified and retaliated in equal measure to the insulting remarks of others. Often he reacted in a hasty, impulsive manner, without reflecting on the issue at hand. In spite of this emotional impulsiveness, he admitted that he was emotionally reticent and had difficulties in sharing his innermost thoughts and feelings with others, was worried about others' opinion of him and had a tendency to brood over things. He was sensitive and empathic as well as oversensitive and reflexive at times. Emotional recovery was reported to be poor and he was unable to respond to the practical demands of the situation. The happy event reported concerned his success in the High School exam. He felt sad and distressed when ever he came across a poor person.

On the School Anxiety scale his fears extended to teachers and exams. He also feared being ridiculed and humiliated in class, and not getting good marks. As for career-related worries, he was apprehensive that he would unable to get the job he aspired for and lamented the lack of career guidance and the paucity of information pertaining to different career options.

He was found to have a poor academic self-concept and described himself mostly in negative terms. He felt he was lazy, non-studious, not planful, less bright, less successful, slow in comprehension and having a weak memory. His positive academic attributes included being confident, superior to others and good in

Math. He rated his own ability as very poor and his performance as being on par with others. His parents tended to concur with his assessment, but they felt that his ability was less than that of others. On the contrary, his teacher described him in more positive terms rating both his ability and performance as being better than others.

In short, MS found school uninteresting, his teachers and peers were unsupportive and the entire school environment far from congenial. He had low academic motivation but cherished academic dreams. He showed less emotional control and was reserved in emotional matters. His academic self-concept was poor and he perceived his ability to be low and performance average. His parents rated him poorly as well. Surprisingly his teachers saw him in a more positive light and rated his ability and performance as better than others.

Case Study VIII

MA is a student of Class IX of School E (ID # 001). On the SPM he scored 14 (Grade V-Intellectually defective). In the previous year's Annual exam he got 65.7 per cent (Level 2) with 78.5 per cent in Arithmetic. This discrepancy in his ability and performance led to his placement in the *Moderate Overachiever's* group.

He found school very interesting, teachers, appreciative, supportive and infusing confidence in students. He did not however, have a very positive image of his school, rating its discipline as harsh and punitive. Teachers were seen as caring and understanding regarding the problems of students. However, they were also seen as being unfair and inconsistent in their evaluation and implementation of disciplinary rules. The peer group was also perceived as being less supportive.

He was found to be academically motivated. Though he reported feeling good when he did not study, he did not find studies a burden and was intrinsically involved in his studies and was less influenced by negative incentives. Though he wished to be thorough in all subjects, surprisingly he did not aspire to get a good position in class.

On the Affect scale, emotional balance was found to be inadequate. He admitted that he was easily provoked to anger and then lost control. He also retaliated in equal measure to the offensive remarks of others often in a hasty, impulsive manner without considering the matter fully and was often envious of the success of others. He could share his innermost thoughts and feelings with others. Emotional recovery was found to be good and negative feelings did not persist. He was sensitive and empathic toward others but not oversensitive. At times, he reported that he was unable to assess a situation objectively and respond to the demands of the situation. No specific happy or sad events were disclosed by him.

He was low on School Anxiety but was somewhat apprehensive of not performing as well as his peers in exams. On Career Worries, he was concerned that he may be unable to attain the job he aspired. He felt that his studies would enhance his job prospects but he bemoaned the lack of adequate career-related information.

MA's academic self-concept was very positive. He described himself as hardworking, studious, planful, bright, successful, sharp in comprehension, having a good memory, confident, superior to others and good in Math. He, however, rated his ability and performance as average. His parents' ratings were similar and they also used the same positive adjectives while describing him. They also felt that he was capable of doing better. His teacher's assessment was more realistic. His teacher described him in negative terms. They rated his ability and performance as average and felt that his performance exceeded his ability.

In summary, MA had a positive view of his school and teachers. He desired to acquire expert knowledge in all subjects. He had inadequate emotional control, was emotionally impulsive, at times reckless. He was open in emotional expression but unable to respond to the practical demands of the situation. While both he and his parents had a positive view of his academic abilities, his teacher viewed him negatively.

Case Study IX

MM (ID # 036) is a student of Class XI of School E. He scored 57 on the SPM (Grade I, Intellectually Superior). In his half-yearly exams his overall percentage was 12.3 per cent (Arithmetic per cent not available) while in the previous year's exam he got 51 per cent (Level 4) with 48 per cent in Math. Hence MM was categorized as an *Extreme Underachiever.*

MM did not have a very positive view of his school or its academic activities. Teachers were seen as unsupportive but were still appreciated as was the school's disciplinary practices. Teachers were reported to being less critical but at the same time they tended to be partial toward certain students. The peer group was perceived as being supportive. He was complimentary about the classrooms, the biology laboratory facilities and the instructional techniques used by teachers. However, he was critical of teachers coercing students to join their coaching classes and also deplored the practice of collecting money from students to celebrate Independence and Republic days. He expressed his dislike of the Vice-Principal of the school.

He obtained high scores on the Academic Motivation scale. He was unable to concentrate at length on his studies but did not find academic pursuits irksome. He was intrinsically motivated, was unaffected by negative incentives and aspired to do well in studies.

On the Affect scale, emotional balance was found to be adequate. He was somewhat impulsive and hasty in his reactions in emotion-provoking situations. He admitted to being easily aroused to anger and reacted hastily to the offensive remarks of others. He was emotionally reserved and reticent and was hesitant in discussing his innermost thoughts and feelings with others. He was bothered by other's opinion of him and negative emotions tended to persist. He was sensitive and empathic to others, at times being oversensitive as well. Though he had a tendency to brood he also reported that he was able to recover from his negative moods quickly and could respond to the practical demands of the situation. He reported happiness when his father presented him with a computer as a reward for being successful in the High School exams. As a consequence, he put in more intensive efforts to improve his performance in English and Math. As far as the sad event is concerned, it focused on his nephew being afflicted with jaundice. The latter had to be hospitalized and the doctors gave up all hope of his recovering. At that point MM resolved to become a doctor and to treat patients with severe ailments.

MM was found to have a high degree of school anxiety. He reported fear of exams, of teachers, of being ridiculed and humiliated in class and of not being able to obtain good marks. He also felt the burden of high parental expectations, as they hoped for a result, he felt he was incapable of achieving. On the Career Worries scale he deplored the lack of career-related information and was worried that he would not get the job he desired. However, he did report that his present studies would brighten his career prospects.

MM's academic self-concept was generally negative. He used the most unflattering of terms to describe himself. Thus he felt that he was less bright, less successful, slow in comprehension, inferior to others and weak in Math. The positive adjectives he used for himself were that he was hardworking, studious, planful and had a good memory. In addition, he reported that he did well in Biology. He rated his ability and performance as better than others. His parents felt he had average ability and performance and described his academic attributes in a similar negative manner. His teachers on the other hand, described him in more positive terms but rated his ability and performance as average.

In summary, MM found school less interesting and teachers less supportive. However, he set high educational goals for himself. He was emotionally reticent, though impulsive in emotional reactivity. He had a high degree of school anxiety and reported considerable parental pressure to excel. His parents and teachers perceived his ability and performance as average. Paradoxically, MM himself, felt he had better ability and performance but described his academic traits negatively.

Case Study X

QN (ID # 011) is a student of Class IX of School E. His SPM

scores were 43 (Grade III, Intellectually Average). In his half-yearly exams he got 60.6 per cent with 72 per cent in Arithmetic, and in his previous annual exam, he got 82 per cent (Level 1) with 85 per cent in Arithmetic. With Level 1 performance and Grade III ability, QN was placed in the *Moderate Overachiever's* group.

He found school interesting and teachers less supportive. On the positive side, teachers were seen as impartial in their evaluation of students and implementation of disciplinary measures as well as infusing confidence in their students. His school, in his eyes was not very impressive but he did appreciate the emphasis which was placed on discipline and its role in character building. The peer group was seen as less supportive. He praised the biology laboratory facilities and the classes on religious instruction which were unique to his school. He also expressed the view that teaching methods and the pedagogy of instruction required change.

QN's Academic Motivation was found to be very high. He found studies stimulating and challenging, they were neither a burden or irksome to him. He was, however, unable to sustain attention for a long period of time. He was deeply committed and involved with his studies and was less affected by negative incentives. He aspired to do well in studies.

On the Affect scale he was found to be emotionally balanced. He was at the same time reticent in sharing his deepest thoughts and feelings with others. He was not very sensitive to the feelings of others but acknowledged being reflexive. Emotional recovery was found to be good. He did not brood over things and could respond to the functional demands of the situation. A happy event recounted by him related to India's victory over Pakistan in the World Cup. Getting poor marks (36%) in a subject in his half-yearly exams was a distressing event for him.

On the School Anxiety scale, he was fearful at the possibility of being ridiculed and humiliated in front of others. On the Career Worries scale, he pointed out that both career-related information and career guidance were in short supply in his school.

He had a positive academic self-concept. His positive academic attributes were that he was hardworking, studious, planful, bright, quick in comprehension, confident, superior to others and good in Math. On the other hand, he also stated that he was less successful than others and had a poor memory. He rated his ability as being better and his performance as being far superior to others. His parents described him in a more balanced manner using both positive and negative terms. They thought his ability and performance were better than others but felt that he was capable of doing better. His teacher's ratings were similar to those given by his parents. In general, his teacher rated his academic traits more positively.

In summary, QN found school interesting and teachers less supportive but he continued to cherish hopes of excelling in studies. He had adequate emotional control, but was reserved and hesitant to share his emotional experiences with others. QN, his parents and teachers all had a positive view of his academic abilities. QN, himself, rated his academic abilities highly and his performance as superior.

Case Study XI

SK (ID # 024) is a student of Class IX of School B. His SPM scores were 51 indicating above average intelligence (Grade II). Contrary to expectation, he obtained 38 per cent in his half-yearly exams with 46 per cent in Arithmetic. In the previous annual examination he got 45.5 per cent (Level 5) with 18 per cent in Arithmetic. Hence SK was categorized as an *Extreme Underachiever.*

On the School Environment scale, SK found school to be very interesting. Teachers were seen as being less supportive but fair and unbiased in their interactions with students. There was obvious pride in the school, in particular its discipline was much appreciated. As to the three best aspects of his school, he reiterated his appreciation of the strict disciplinary practices observed in school. The teachers and infrastructural facilities were also praiseworthy. Regarding those aspects of school that required change, he listed rampant indiscipline among the students and teachers.

Academic motivation was high in SK. He did not find studies to be irksome and once he got down to study, his involvement was total. Negative incentives sometimes led to a decrement in effort and he aimed to do very well in studies.

On the Affect scale, SK was emotionally balanced even though he admitted to losing control when enraged. He was neither too open nor reserved in expressing his emotions and negative feeling states did not persist for long. He was empathic and sensitive towards others. He was not hasty in his reactions, was not overwhelmed by emotions and emotional recovery was adequate. His behaviour was guided by the situation. A happy event as recalled by him was when his parents gave him a vehicle (details not specified) as a reward for doing well in the exams. The sad event related to the death of his pet dog and he reported feelings of sadness and despair.

On the School Anxiety scale he was found to be fearful and apprehensive of not being able to get good marks in the examination. He also admitted that there was considerable pressure because of high parental expectations. A moderate degree of School Anxiety was evident. Career worries were not excessive, but he felt that he would not be able to get the job he coveted. As far as his career was concerned, there was no parental pressure to pursue a specific career to the exclusion of others. He was doubtful as to whether his present studies would lead to career opportunities.

SK's academic self-concept was generally positive. He saw himself as hard-working, planful, quick in comprehension, confident, superior to others and having a good memory. However, he also described himself as being less bright, less successful, not studious and weak in Math. He rated his performance and ability as being better than others. His parents described him in more negative terms and also rated his ability and performance as being inferior to others. His Math teacher also rated him poorly on almost all academic traits. He was of the view that SK's ability was at par with that of other students but his performance was not commensurate with his ability.

In summary, SK viewed school as interesting, his teachers as being less supportive but continued to nurture high educational goals. In the emotional sphere he was found to be well balanced but lost control when angry. He viewed his academic abilities more positively as compared with his parents. His teacher felt that he had average ability but his performance was below average.

Case Study XII

RG is a student of Class IX of School C (ID # 003). His SPM score was 40 (Grade III, Intellectually Average). He obtained 81.6 per cent (Level 1) in the previous year's annual examination with 91.9 per cent in Arithmetic (Half-yearly examination marks were not available). Due to this obvious difference between ability and performance he was placed in the *Moderate Overachiever's* group.

On the School Environment scale he found school to be interesting and teachers moderately supportive. He liked the teachers and felt that they instilled confidence in their students and were consistent in enforcing disciplinary rules. However, they were also seen as partial, critical and indifferent to the problems of students. He appreciated the discipline practiced in school though he was not really proud of his school. He enjoyed extracurricular activities in school but criticized the practice of taking I.Q. tests as was done in his school.

RG had a very high degree of academic motivation. He did not find studies irksome. He had an intrinsic involvement in academic pursuits. Negative incentives, such as low marks spurred him to greater effort in the concerned subject. He set high academic goals for himself.

On the Affect scale his emotional balance was found to be adequate. He admitted to being easily provoked to anger and retaliated fully to the offensive remarks of others. He had some difficulty in sharing his thoughts and feelings with others and was also bothered by other's opinion of him. He was moderately sensitive to the feelings of others and at times was oversensitive himself. His emotional recovery was good, though he tended to brood over things. He was not overwhelmed by his emotional state and was able to respond to the practical demands of the situation. The happy event reported pertained to his winning the first prize in a quiz competition. The sad event was the passing away of his uncle. He was very upset and disturbed by this event.

School anxiety was found to be moderately high. He was fearful of examinations, of being ridiculed in class, and of not getting good marks. RG had minimal career worries.

As far as his academic self-concept was concerned, he described himself as being hard-working, studious, planful, quick in comprehension, and good in Math. His negative traits were listed as being less bright, less successful, nervous and inferior to others. He perceived his ability as being average and his performance as being poorer than others. His parents described him in more positive terms and rated his ability and performance as being better than others. However, they also felt that his performance was below his ability. His teacher also shared his parents' views, though he described RG in more negative terms and rated his ability and performance as being average.

In summary RG found school interesting and teachers moderately supportive. He had high educational aspirations. His emotional control was adequate and he had some difficulty in sharing his thoughts and feelings with others. A moderate degree of school anxiety was reported. He rated his ability as average and his performance as being inferior to others. His parents rated his ability and performance positively, while his teacher had a more negative view of his academic abilities and rated his ability and performance as being average.

Case Study XIII

AP (ID # 042) is a student of Class XI of School A. He obtained a score of 51 on SPM (Grade II, Above Average Intelligence). In his Half-Yearly exams he got 31 per cent (Arithmetic percentage, not available) while in his previous year's Annual exams he obtained 43.4 per cent (Level 5) with 33 per cent in Arithmetic. Hence, AP was placed in the *Extreme Underachiever's* group.

He found school very interesting but teachers less supportive, he had a very positive view of his school being obviously proud of being a part of the institution. Teachers were seen as being critical, partial and indifferent to the problems of students. He found that the rules and regulations of school were harsh and restrictive. Peer group was seen as being less supportive. He appreciated the disciplinary practices in school and the systematic and regular teaching. He did feel that teachers were capable and efficient. He criticized the paucity of extracurricular activities and felt some teachers were too strict.

Academic motivation was found to be adequate. He did not find studies irksome. Study involvement was not high. He was affected by negative aspirations and had a high aspiration level.

On the Affect scale, emotional control was found to be adequate. He retaliated in equal measure to the offensive remarks of others. He was open in sharing his intimate thoughts and feelings with others but was always concerned about what others thought of him. His negative feelings tended to persist. He was sensitive and empathic towards others, sometimes being oversensitive as well. His emotional recovery was adequate but he tended to brood over matters. He could act in accordance with the practical demands of the situation. The happy event concerned his obtaining 74 per cent in English in his High School examination. The event which made him sad was the death of his grandmother. He reported being very upset after this tragedy, losing interest in all activities.

As for school anxiety, AP was fearful of being ridiculed and humiliated in class in front of others. On the Career Worries scale he reported apprehension that he would not get the job he sought. He also felt that his present studies would enhance his career prospects.

AP in general had a low academic self-concept. He described himself as lazy, not studious, not planful, less bright and successful and weak in Math. At the same time he felt that he was quick in comprehension, confident, superior to others and had a good memory. He added that he could not study for more than an hour at a time. He rated his ability as poor and his performance as being inferior to others. His parents described him in even more negative terms and rated his performance as being poorer and his ability as being better than others. Significantly, his teacher uniformly described his academic traits in a negative manner, but rated his ability and performance as average.

In summary, AP had a positive view of his school but thought negatively about his teachers. He had high educational aspirations. He had adequate emotional control and had a tendency to brood. He was low on school anxiety and career worries. He had a poor academic self-concept and rated both his ability and performance as being poor compared to others. His parents also rated his abilities in a similar, negative manner but felt he had better ability. His teacher had an extremely negative view of AP's academic abilities but felt his ability and performance were average.

Case Study XIV

SS (ID # 019) is a student of Class IX of School A. She had an SPM score of 44 (Grade III, Intellectually Average). In her Half Yearly exams she got 74 per cent with 84 per cent in Math while in the previous year's Annual exam she got 78 per cent (Level 1) with 70 per cent in Math. As a result of this difference between her ability and performance SS was placed in the *Moderate Overachiever's* group.

She found school to be very interesting. She perceived her teachers as supportive, appreciative, infusing confidence in students and thinking positively of them. Teachers also fostered a sense of pride and belongingness in the school, were fair and unbiased in their evaluation, consistent in their implementation of disciplinary rules and attentive to the personal problems of students. However, she did point out that teachers tended to neglect weak students. The peer group was perceived as unhelpful and unsupportive. She appreciated the library facilities and the various competitions held in school. She observed that sports were less encouraged and that the science laboratories were far from adequate. She also felt that non-academically inclined students vitiated the school environment.

SS's academic motivation was found to be very high. She found studies to be neither a burden nor irksome. However, she was less involved in studies. She was not influenced by negative incentives and had high educational aspirations.

She had just about adequate emotional control. She was easily provoked to anger, retaliated in equal measure to the offensive behaviour of others and was envious of others' success. She was emotionally reticent, was always worried about what others thought of her and had a tendency to brood over things. She reported being sensitive and empathic towards others, at times being over-sensitive as well. Emotional recovery was good and she acted in accordance with the situation. The happy event was when she came fifth in class. She was very happy and "free of tension" due to this success. As for the sad event she reported being very tense and disturbed when she was isolated by other family members because of the stand she took on a family matter.

She had a moderate degree of school anxiety. She was apprehensive of being ridiculed and humiliated in class and felt that her parents expected results exceeding her ability. As far as Career Worries are concerned she did not think that the present course of studies would enhance her career prospects and was doubtful if she would get a job of her choice. She also felt that she lacked adequate career-related information.

She had a generally positive academic self-concept and felt she was hardworking, studious, planful, bright, successful and confident. At the same time this positive picture was tempered by the fact that she also felt that she was inferior to others, weak in Math, slow in comprehension and having a poor memory. She added that she did not give up easily and had the quality of persistence. She had a realistic perception of her ability as being relatively less than others but her performance being better than that of others. Her parents described her in extremely positive terms, rating both her ability and performance as being far superior to others. Her parents also felt that she achieved beyond her ability. Her teacher also subscribed to this positive view of SS's academic traits and rated both her ability and performance as being better than others and her performance as being consistent with her ability.

In summary, SS had a very positive view of her school and teachers and had high educational aspirations. She had adequate emotional control and was reticent on emotional matters. She had a moderate amount of school anxiety. Her positive perception of her own academic abilities was generally endorsed by her parents and teacher. She was also realistic in her assessment and rated her performance as exceeding her ability. Her parents and teachers on the other had viewed her ability and performances as being at par and being far superior to that of others.

Unifying Themes: Convergences and Points of Departure

From the large sample of underachievers (N = 116), seven cases of underachievers and seven cases of moderate over-achievers were selected for an in-depth individual-focused examination and analysis using the case-study method. Based on these 14 cases it is possible to identify certain common themes and points of similarity and convergence within each group. The differences between these two extreme groups will also be dealt with. The aim is to present an integrative analysis.

First, it is evident that even though questionnaire data was the basis of the case studies, some of the information obtained (in particular Affect scale data and ratings of academic abilities) is more meaningful when handled in a qualitative manner.

As far as perception of school environment was concerned, most of the overachievers found school interesting and stimulating. In contrast, only 50 per cent of the underachievers found school interesting while the rest were either indifferent in their attitude towards school or found school tiresome and uninteresting. Almost all the overachievers perceived the teachers to be supportive. The underachievers, on the other hand viewed their teachers as being non-supportive and non-facilitative. Six of the seven underachievers studied found school discipline to be harsh, inconsistent and punitive. However, only two of the overachievers found the discipline followed in school to be strict and one rated it as being inconsistent. Almost 50 per cent of the cases in both the groups perceived the peer group as being non-supportive. This may be explained in terms of academic and personal rivalry issues which are at their strongest for students in these classes.

Again though both groups had sound academic motivation and aspired to do well, the underachievers were frequently discouraged by negative incentives (poor marks, less reinforcement from teachers, fear of public humiliation and ridicule). Overachievers were highly motivated, felt their teachers were supportive and reinforcing and also experienced less parental pressures. It was also found that overachievers had an intrinsic involvement in their studies while at least 50 per cent of the underachievers lacked intrinsic study involvement.

The Affect index seems to be an important factor and seems to have clear implications for academic achievement and underachievement. This was a hitherto, unrevealed effect as the quantitative analysis did not show many significant differences. For instance, underachievers (almost 75%) were emotionally reticent and reserved and were unable to share experiences and to express anger and resentment. In the case of overachievers about 50 per cent were found to be reticent on emotional matters. This is significant in light of the finding that underachievers have a passive-aggressive behavioural style. Underachievers were also found to be over-sensitive and had poor emotional recovery. Over-achievers, on the other hand showed greater emotional fortitude and recovery. It was also found that almost all the underachievers tended to brood over their past failures and lapses. This tendency was less prevalent in the over-achievers group. The over-achievers had better emotional control, were less muted in their emotional expression and were less engulfed by their emotions.

School anxiety was found to be relatively higher in the underachiever group. However, both groups had one enduring fear: that of being ridiculed and humiliated in front of others. Worries regarding the future were also pervasive in both groups, in particular both underachievers and overachievers felt that all their academic efforts would be wasted as they would be unable to get the job they desired and aspired for. Another lacunae deeply felt by both groups of students pertained to the lack of adequate career-guidance and career-related information.

Again, as in the case of quantitative data analysis, Academic self-concept and the corresponding appraisals of parents' and teachers were found to be significant. For overachievers, their self-assessment was more realistic and accurate and often in line with the objective measures of ability (SPM). While overachievers were rated more positively, both their parents and teachers rated underachievers, in spite of their outstanding intellectual ability more negatively. In most cases teachers had an average to poor perception of underachieving students. This again, substantiates the fact that teacher expectancies play a significant role in academic outcomes.

At least 50 per cent of the underachievers had a negative academic self-concept. Only one of the overachievers rated their academic abilities negatively.

In view of the magnitude of the problem, the next section will focus on interventions.

Chapter 7

INTERVENTIONS

The previous section ended with case studies. In this chapter, a case study based on a clinical encounter with an underachiever is being presented, as it illustrates several basic and important issues concerned with interventions for underachievers. This case study is based on the clinical work of one of the *Authors (KT).*

SR, 16 years old, a student of class XI of the Commerce stream in one of the leading schools of Allahabad was referred to me in April 1998. She had shown gradual decline in academic performance from class VI onwards. Both her parents were successful professionals: her mother, a doctor at a prestigious local hospital and her father, an engineer at a leading public sector undertaking. Her younger brother was reported to be very bright, doing well in academics and an all-rounder as well.

SR was reported to be introverted, sensitive, irritable would often burst into tears and expressed feelings of inferiority. She was also reported to be affectionate and caring, but very private and rarely expressed her feelings. Parents conceded that initially they had high expectations from her and would often make unflattering comparisons with her younger brother.

SR was so much in the mould of the classic underachiever whose underachievement stemmed from a fear of failure and comparisons with successful parents and siblings that I administered the Rorschach Inkblot test to get further insights into her psyche. The Rorschach protocol showed an underdeveloped at times fragmented self, less responsivity to emotional stimuli probably as consequence of early rejection experiences as well as the fact that emotional factors and tensions had interfered with the constructive use of intellectual abilities. She was also found to be emotionally withdrawn, rarely expressing emotional and affectional impulses.

After this assessment SR and her mother (who had made the initial consultation) did not met me till October 1998, in spite of some efforts on my part to share assessment findings with them. Apparently, in between, the ICSE results were declared and SR's results were better than expected (close to 60%).

In October 1998, SR's mother again asked me to help out. I administered some more tests including an ability test, SPM, where SR got a score of 48, Grade II, interpreted as being definitely above average in intellectual functioning. At this time as well, SR was friendly but would clam up when academic issues were discussed. She also disclosed two recurrent dreams, which were indicative of her turbulent inner life. She often dream of 9-10 *chudail* (witches) with blue, green and yellow faces peering at her from the window while one friendly witch helped her to hide under the table. The second dream focused on someone pursuing her while she was running up a flight of stairs and losing her footing and falling down.

I started work with SR with the following goals: reduction of anxiety and fear, enhancing self-image (*vis-à-vis* parents and brother), changing her attitude to academic tasks (nervous, apprehensive, expectancy of failure) and used a number of cognitive behavioural techniques. SR was co-operative but her parents were uninvolved and detached from this process.

SR voluntarily withdrew from therapy in November 1998, as term-examinations were imminent. Her mother again contacted me in February 1999 and for the first time divulged the extent of SR's academic problems. In October, SR had failed in 2 subjects, in February her marks had plummeted to a new low (18%) and failure extended to 4 subjects. Her mother sought an interview with the class teacher who was harsh and critical and dismissive of SR as a "hopeless case". In school itself, when her mother spoke to SR, she reported that this state of affairs had been continuing for the past 6 months, with the teachers constantly scolding and criticising her.

This case study was presented not only because it clinically confirmed and substantiated many of the significant findings of this study (emotional reticence, emotional over-sensitivity, poor emotional recovery in underachievers, teachers being harsh and non-facilitative and having low expectations); not because it showcased the grave human costs involved (the emotional distress to the underachiever and her family), but because there is an important lesson to be learned, a significant learning to be derived. Without the active co-operation and involvement of the concerned student, parents and teachers, without a consensus in terms of shared goals and objectives any programme of intervention can be sabotaged by the key players in this school drama.

Two other considerations are important and serve as imperatives to action. It is almost a truism that academic problems in particular underachievement can lead to distress, covert or overt. Emotional distress influences cognitive processes, which in turn lead to subsequent academic problems. Thus, children who experience predominantly negative emotions sometimes show mood-congruent biases of memory and attention (Gotlib & MacLeod, 1997) that can affect academic functioning. For instance, feelings of distress can activate negative academic motivational beliefs in memory during learning activities. For sad or anxious students, this biasing may be reflected in pervasive worries about incompetence in learning situations, whereas angry students may perseverate on presumed hostile attentions of others (Dweck & Wortman, 1982; Gotlib & MacLeod, 1997). Negative, mood-induced biases of this sort can divert the investment of psychological resources into self-protective goals and coping efforts rather than into academic mastery goals and learning strategies (Boekarts, 1993). Reduced attentional, cognitive and emotional investments in learning can precipitate subsequent academic problems. A second, related process by which negative mood can influence academic functioning involves the biasing effect of mood on attention. Distress-induced attentional biases operate to filter out information that is at odds with any particular, prevailing negative emotional state (Segal & Cloitre, 1993). Thus students experiencing high levels of either internalized or externalized distress in academic settings may discount positive experiences (e.g., moments of academic success or support by others), and focus instead on mood-consistent experiences (e.g., difficulties in learning), thereby maintaining the original negative emotional state. The reciprocal nature of these processes helps to explain why many students with academic difficulties such as underachievement also show emotional difficulties, and vice versa.

In the area of interventions, a fair reading of the literature suggests that no single intervention technique has succeeded for the majority of students with a particular school. Phillips (1983) recommends a conceptual rather than a prescriptive approach to interventions in schools. This approach includes the remedial model, which involves initiating help when the student is experiencing achievement-related problems, the developmental model in which attempts are made to identify incipient or mild achievement-related problems and intervening to forestall further problems; and the preventive model where the goal is to forestall the onset of academic-related dysfunctions. Wiener's (1983) intervention approaches for underachievers varies with the nature of the particular socio-cultural or psychological factors that are contributing to their school learning problems. For instance, for passive-aggressive underachievement, brief counselling with parents or with the underachiever himself/herself was deemed appropriate.

Based on the quantitative data obtained in this study and following an analysis of case studies, the general findings of this study showed that underachievers generally perceived their school environment positively; however, teachers were seen as being partial and biased and also perceived as being non-supportive and non-facilitative of academic pursuits. Underachievers also tended to become easily discouraged by negative incentives. Their perception of their own academic and learning abilities was poor, but significantly, parents and to a much greater degree teachers rated them even more negatively. As far as basic emotional skills were concerned underachievers tended to be emotionally reticent, they were over-sensitive and had poor emotional recovery. These findings provide sufficient bases for the interventions, which are being consequently proposed. A cautionary note is required here. These interventions are in the form of general strategic plans and proposals. Their actual implementation would require close consideration and attention to the particularities and unique features of the school system focused upon including the school climate, the ideological bases, the educational ambience and ethos, pedagogical practices, teachers and a host of other associated variables. It is also important to remember that although schools have long been recognized as efficient and cost-effective sites for efforts to promote developmental competence and for identifying and redressing achievement-related difficulties, school-based programmes often prove difficult to implement and sustain (Durlak, 1995).

Other approaches are based on goal theory which posits that achievement goals can be influenced by classroom incentive systems, either to the benefit or detriment of achievement (Covington, 2000). The first system assumes that students are optimally motivated by there being fewer rewards than players in the learning game, i.e. turning students into competitors. This model derives much of its justification from the view that considers motivation as an enabling factor, i.e. the means to superior performance. The second broad system is an alternative to the competitive model and assumes that motivation is optimal when there exists an abundance of payoffs for learning. These payoffs may be tangible, extrinsic rewards as well as intrinsic sources of satisfaction.

As this study has highlighted underachievement is a grave and pervasive problem requiring urgent and immediate intervention. As it affects a substantial portion of the school-going population (47% of the sample studied was found to be underachievers) the first-level interventions would be at the *school level.*

Here dissemination of information seems to be important and preparing information packages pertaining to the prevalence and magnitude of the problem could do this. School administrations principals and teachers would be the primary recipients of this information, but media attention and coverage could also highlight the severity of the problem. Going back to the schools that participated in this study and providing them with specific feedback regarding the achievement status and other detailed results pertaining to their students can be the first step. An alternative strategy would be to invite the participating schools for a workshop, with the primary aim of sharing the results of the study but also seeking to establish collaborative ventures with them for dealing with the problem.

It would also be feasible to work with different levels of school personnel (for example, principals, other administrative staff and teachers) to evolve strategies for enhancing the learning environment and emotional climate of schools. In other words, it seems imperative to alert, sensitize and draw the attention of the entire school system as to what is happening to students in their precincts and to convince them that the problems of underachievement need to be immediately faced and tackled. Depending on the reactions of schools, any-one school can be the focus of a planned intervention package, which may be introduced initially on an experimental basis and subject to periodic evaluation and revision. This package would then serve as a model for planning and implementing interventions in other schools as well. Also schools may seek additional inputs in the form of large-scale surveys to determine the true incidence of underachievement. It needs to be pointed out here that only 50 students were sampled from each school. Using the Index of Underachievement and other selected measures it would be possible to devise small screening measures, which could be used to identify underachievement.

At the school-level as well, the need for school psychologists and counsellors seems imperative. Again, here institutional support is required at the school management level to create posts for counsellors and to promote and facilitate comprehensive, balanced school counselling programmes. In view of the immediacy and magnitude of the problem of underachievement, the first activities of the school counsellor may focus on identifying underachievers, attempting to obtain a personalised view of each case and to act as a liaison between home and schools, between parents and teachers and together with them evolve strategies to counter the damaging effects of underachievement. At a later stage, the more traditional functions of assessment, facilitating life-skill development, career development and personal and social development may be the focus of the school counsellor's efforts. In other words, the first intervention strategy being proposed is to first sensitise and then to mobilise the entire school system to respond as a functional unit to cope with the pervasive problem of underachievement. Once the severity of the problem is recognised and accepted at the school systemic level, other specific interventions can be planned and implemented.

The focus of the next set of interventions would be *teachers.* As stated earlier underachievers in particular, tended to perceive their teachers as being partial, non-supportive and non-facilitative of their academic efforts. Teachers, in turn generally viewed the academic and learning abilities of underachievers in a negative manner, which generated negative expectancies. Jackson (2001) has recommended the use of a pedagogy of confidence for reversing underachievement. When teachers practice this pedagogy they do not doubt the potential of their students, and switch their instructional focus from what has to be taught to how to maximize learning. Through this practice, a teacher uses an instructional model that guides the development of his or her teaching methods, the selection of learning strategies, and the design of assessments, which in turn accelerates and enriches the learning of students. The model has three core concepts that act as instructional objectives: self-discovery, mediated learning and literacy enrichment. Self-discovery is important because two of the greatest motivators of learning are confidence in one's abilities and self-worth. Both strengthen the sense of identity that is critical to developing the motivation to achieve. Self-discovery is a process of reflection that is built into instruction as a learning ritual, connecting to students on both an affective level and a cognitive one. It is designed around a set of questions that the students must think through and react to with concrete responses. The affective level addresses a student's sense of personal identity. The cognitive level of self-discovery is a cycle of reflection. Mediated learning (Feuerstein, 1982) is an interactive process that bonds the teacher and student in a nurturing relationship. The goal of mediated learning is to elicit from the students a personal motivation for learning. The teacher engages the student around purposely selected activities that build their confidence by guiding them in discussion to critically analyze tasks and identify relevant connections and applications to their personal experiences. Finally, literacy enhancement is the key to empowering students. It is the primary focus of mediated learning and the context in which the "codes of power" are developed. Eisner (1994) described it as an individual's ability to construct, create, and communicate meaning in many forms.

Here the need to organise workshops for teachers and to sensitise them to their impact on students' academic success and performance also assumes salience. Here, the Department of Psychology's on going programme of teacher workshops could be the forum for a discussion related to issues of achievement and underachievement. At least 3 of the authors of this book *(RCT, MV & KT)* have been involved in these workshops. Further, schools also need to plan programmes to enthuse and sustain the motivation of teachers.

Finally, *parents* are also essential components in any intervention programme. In particular, parents of underachievers need to be active participants in any intervention programme that seeks to deal with the problem of underachievement. Again, here it is believed that it is the school psychologist who can mediate and act as a liaison between parents and teachers to ensure their concerted involvement and co-operation in attaining common goals. Mutuality of efforts and goals would go a long way in ensuring the success of the intervention programme.

One of the major findings of the study related to different patterns of emotional functioning observed in under- and over-achievers. It is evident that at least some of the proposed intervention strategies should include aspects of *affective education* and what are now referred to as *emotional literacy* programme. For example, affective education programme include the Human Development

Programme (Bessell & Palamares, 1969) which can be a part of the classroom curriculum. This programme utilises the "magic circle" as the tool to achieving positive and creative emotional and social development. Emotional literacy programmes (Goleman, 1995, 1998) have also been developed with the aim of increasing emotional self-awareness, effective management of emotions and harnessing emotions in a more productive manner. Studies have shown that emotional literacy programmes can lead to an improvement in children's academic achievement scores and school performance.

Intervention (B)

Another *Intervention Package (B)* has been prepared by one of the *authors (CS)* using the human resource development perspective. This is being included as it offers a different perspective, although there are obvious similarities and correspondence of views.

Based on the results of the study, a framework for a set of Intervention Programmes is presented which includes the following:

- Accelerating progress towards the institution's mission goals, and even re-defining goals,
- A developmental balanced approach to school counselling,
- Classroom guidance,
- Small group counselling,
- Individual counselling,
- Teacher and parent involvement.

The proposed framework addresses various issues, concerns and the objectives of the target group. Hence, before developing these suggested frameworks into full-fledged intervention programmes, we advise the concerned authorities to consult experts and consider the immediate reality for each institution (i.e. schools), as they are distinctly unique.

The suggested frameworks are as follows :

Framework I: Accelerating progress towards the Institution's mission goals, and even re-defining goals.

Framework II: To promote comprehensive, balanced school counselling programmes conducted by trained counsellors capable of meeting both remedial and developmental goals for adolescents living in a pluralistic society.
Framework III: (for) Teachers.
Framework IV: (for) Parents.

FRAMEWORK-I

Accelerating progress towards the institution's mission, goals, and even re-defining goals.

Until recently institutions such as schools in India, neither considered it relevant nor found it necessary to formulate and spell-out mission statements.

Objectives

Defining institutional mission and putting it down in the form of a "mission-statement" is a recent practice. Hence there is a need to look at the purpose of institution with respect to two types of objectives:

Mission-oriented Objectives

Social and institutional development commitments which determine the direction in which the institution seems to be going.

Objectives Related to Efficiency of the Organisation

Use of resources…human, financial, and material.

The variables to be considered by the proposed framework are:

- Inputs, in terms of
- People [i.e. members of the institution: the Principal, the management, and teachers], and their competencies.

- Processes related to mission or goals
- The relevance, the needs of the beneficiaries, changes in culture, values and such other soft variables.

Methodology

Listed below are a set of methodologies, which are proposed in this section. For each institution, the selection of the prescribed methods will vary, as the requirement may be, and will be selected by an expert.

To initiate the process of evaluating the institutional goals and even re-defining them, questions like *"why are we doing this and what are we doing"*, could be the starting point of the reflection process. This could lead to re-examining mission statements and even check the ability of the mission in terms of the need to broaden its scope to accommodate the changing environment.

Reflections, if carried out in time can help, to control and tighten such situations, link the mission to current situations, re-build confidence and remove frustrations.

The proposed methods are as follows:

- Workshops
- Group discussions
- Brainstorming sessions
- Information collection through the study of records, old documents

FRAMEWORK-II

To promote comprehensive, balanced school counselling programs conducted by trained counsellors capable of meeting both remedial and developmental goals for adolescents living in a pluralistic society.

Goals*:* To translate the institutional mission and purposes, into action oriented programmes.

The programme components suggested are based on goals that are organised into three areas.

Academic Development Goals

- *Planning and Programming:* The counsellor acts as a liaison between home, school, and community in designing programmes based on needs.
- *Facilitating Instruction Based on Students' Needs:* The counsellor provides instructional consultation through screening, assessment and interpretation of student academic records as an advocate of the whole individual (i.e. student).
- *Intervention:* The counsellor provides interventions on school adjustment issues related to the academic success of the student.
- *Assessment:* The counsellor evaluates guidance programme effectiveness related to the student's academic success on an ongoing basis through formal and/or informal means.

Life Skill and Career Development Goals

- *Planning and Programming:* The counsellor facilitates the integration of career awareness and skills development into the curriculum.
- *Facilitating Instruction Based on Student Needs:* The counsellor co-ordinates and assesses enrichment opportunities in the area of life and career development.
- *Intervention:* The counsellor provides and/or co-ordinates career or life skill interventions related to the future successes of the student.
- *Assessment:* The counsellor evaluates guidance programme effectiveness related to career awareness and life skills development on an ongoing basis through formal and/or informal means.

Personal/School Development

- *Planning and Programming:* The counsellor functions as

a positive force in the school, helping to create a climate in which all the students' personal and developmental needs are addressed. The counsellor involves the principal, teachers and parents in this process.

- *Facilitating Instruction Based on Students' Needs:* The counsellor provides consultation in the use of effective strategies in response to student needs as they relate to personal success.
- *Intervention:* The counsellor provides and co-ordinates interventions on personal and social issues affecting the well-being of the student.
- *Assessment:* The counsellor evaluates guidance programme effectiveness related to personal and social success on an ongoing basis through formal and/or informal means.

Functions of the Suggested Balanced Counselling Programme

A set of functions are suggested for the proposed intervention, where each function is a specific professional behaviour aimed at accomplishing stated objectives, contributing to the suggested balanced counselling programme. These sets of functions are focused on enhancing the students' growth and development. They are as follows:

- *Counselling*
- *Curriculum Programming*
- *Consulting*
- *Referral and Co-ordination*
- *Information*
- *Transition Enhancement*
- *Assessment*
- *Accountability*

Special Function

The suggested balanced counselling programme has to attend to the most voiced concern of their respective schools. This concern is related to the issue of *Underachievement.*

The study has shown that *Underachievement* seems to have many causes. Through this study and the suggested programme, counsellors will be in a position to identify the underachieving students.

Hence, the *Goal of this Special Function,* suggested is to enable the counsellors to find ways to respond to the symptoms and causes of the individual and group cases, by involving the services of the teachers and parents.

But the involvement of teachers and parents would presuppose that these two most important members are equipped to deliver their services towards the attainment of the goal.

So in order to equip the teachers and parents, to become active partners, we suggest two frameworks, one each for both the members. This framework could be developed into full-fledged intervention programmes as per the requirements and the available resources of the institutions.

FRAMEWORK-III

Focus: Teachers

The framework suggested for the teachers intends :

- To build, operationalize, implement and disseminate a culture of co-operation and co-ordination with the proposed balanced school counselling programme, and the counsellor.
- To equip them with skills to understand the needs, difficulties and emotional health of the students.
- To develop a close bond, a tradition of interaction with the students and parents.
- To enable them to be sensitive towards their students, who are underachievers and need special assistance.

Issues

The programme suggested addresses the following sets of issues, and would facilitate the process of dissemination, if attended to. They are as follows :

- Strategies developed need to be holistic, as well as culture-specific, with regards to the problems encountered in school settings.
- Teachers, if sensitised, can function effectively with not just one group of students, but many such students every year, as long as they remain in the profession.
- The strategies devised must aim to develop skills in those who are already working actively with students, as they may be better informed about externalising or scholastic problems.
- The focus should not only be on identification and referral but also on intervention (in co-ordination with the school counsellor), by trained teachers.
- The strategies developed should be simple to work with and evaluate, as teachers would be expected to carry out the tasks alongside their normal duties.

Concerns

While devising a programme for the teachers, the institution must keep in cognisance that there are sets of apprehensions, which have been, shared by the teachers. Hence it is important to frame the interventions, according to their respective realities.

- The first and foremost apprehension is that a lot of extra work is going to be foisted on them, with authorities colluding with the outside team.
- The second is that they would be required to attend the programme, whether they like it or not, so they may have fears, anxieties and resentments.
- There may be issues to which the teachers may have a justifiable concern over, such as being overburdened by extra duties.

- The timing of the sessions should be scheduled so as to be mutually convenient to the teachers as well as the management.
- It must be abundantly clear that the teachers should attend the program out of their own choice and not under pressure or compulsion.

Methodology

Listed below are a set of methodologies, which are proposed in this section. Though for each institution, the selection of the prescribed methods will vary, as the requirement may be, and to be selected by an expert. The methods are as follows:

- Workshops
- Group discussions
- Brainstorming sessions
- Problem-solving sessions
- Task-forces

FRAMEWORK IV

Focus : Parents

The framework suggested for the parents intends :

- To build, operationalize, implement and disseminate a culture of co-operation and co-ordination with the teachers and the counsellor.
- To equip them with skills to understand the needs, difficulties and emotional health of their child.
- To develop a close bond, a tradition of interaction with the teacher, child and the counsellor.
- To enable them to be sensitive towards their children, who are underachievers and need special assistance.
- To sensitise them to the need for a balanced school counselling programme.

Issues

The programme suggested address the following sets of issues, and would facilitate the process of dissemination if attended to. As the goal of the programme is to reach out to parents, hence the authorities, teachers and the counsellor should take them into confidence. They are as follows :

- Information about the balanced school counselling programme and their active participation in it to be increased.
- Strategies developed need to be holistic, as well as culture specific, with regards to the problems encountered at home.
- Parents, if sensitised, can understand their child better by helping them overcome their fears, anxieties, and failures.
- The strategies devised must aim to develop skills in those who are already working actively with counsellors, as they may be better informed and sensitive to internalizing.
- The focus should not only be on identification should not only be on identification and referral but also on intervention in co-ordination with school counsellor, and teachers.
- The strategies developed should be simple to work with and evaluate, as parents would be expected to carry out the task alongside there normal duties.

Methodology

Listed below are a set of methodologies, which are proposed in this section. Though for each institution, the prescribed methods will vary, as the requirements may be, and will be selected by an expert.

The methods are as follows :

- Workshops
- Problem-solving Sessions
- Individual Counselling
- Small group Counselling

APPENDICES

APPENDIX–A

रिसर्च-प्रश्नावली

(स्टूडेन्ट्-फ़ॉर्म)

मनोविज्ञान विभाग, इलाहाबाद विश्वविद्यालय एवं सीमैट, इलाहाबाद, जनवरी, 1997

प्रिय छात्रों

आप जानना चाहेंगे कि इस रिसर्च के द्वारा हम क्या पता लगाना चाहते हैं? हमारा मानना है कि ज़्यादातर स्टूडेंट्स अपनी बुद्धि (इंटेलिजैंस) का पूरा प्रयोग नहीं कर पाते हैं, जिसकी वजह से इम्तहानों में वे अपनी आशा से कम अच्छा कर पाते हैं। इस रिसर्च में हम कुछ ऐसे ही कारणों का पता लगाने की कोशिश कर रहे हैं। आप सभी प्रश्नों को ध्यान से पढ़िये और ठीक से सोचकर उनके जवाब दीजिए। आप जितने सच्चे उत्तर देंगे, उतने अधिक इस रिसर्च के सही परिणाम हमें मिलेंगे। आपके उत्तरों के आधार पर हम स्टूडेंट्स की बेहतर मदद कर पाएंगे।

जवाब कैसे दें?

इस प्रश्नावली में 5 भाग हैं। हर भाग में कुछ सवाल/कथन हैं। हर सवाल को ध्यान से पढ़िये और ज्यादातर सवालों के नीचे या सामने एक स्केल दिया गया है जिसको इस्तेमाल करके आपको यह बताना है कि आपके ख़्याल में हर कथन किस हद तक सही है। हर कथन के सामने 5 अंक दिये गए हैं। जैसे:

बहुत कम	कम	न कम न ज़्यादा (बीच का)	ज़्यादा	बहुत ज़्यादा
1	2	3	4	5

- यदि आप पर वह कथन बहुत कम लागू होता है, तब आप 1 को गोले से घेर दीजिए।
- यदि आप पर यह कथन कम लागू होता है, तब आप 2 को गोले से घेर दीजिए।
- यदि आप पर यह कथन न कम न ज़्यादा (बीच का) लागू होता है, तब आप 3 को गोले से घेर दीजिए।
- यदि आप पर यह कथन ज्यादा लागू होता है, तब आप 4 को गोले से घेर दीजिए।
- यदि आप पर यह कथन बहुत ज़्यादा लागू होता है, तब आप 5 को गोले से घेर दीजिए।

भाग–1

इस भाग में आपके स्कूल के बारे में कुछ बातें पूछी जा रही हैं। कहाँ तक सच है कि –

		बहुत कम	कम	न कम न ज़्यादा	ज़्यादा	बहुत ज़्यादा
1.	टीचर हमें अपनी बात कहने का मौका देते हैं।	1	2	3	4	5
2.	हमारे साथी स्टूडेंट्स अपने दिल की बातें एक दूसरे से छिपाते हैं।	1	2	3	4	5
3.	टीचर, स्टूडेन्ट्स की निजी (पर्सनल) कमियों पर कमेन्ट करते है।	1	2	3	4	5
4.	हमारे साथी एक दूसरे की मदद करते हैं।	1	2	3	4	5
5.	स्कूल बड़ा बोरिंग लगता है।	1	2	3	4	5
6.	टीचर हमारी निजी (पर्सनल) समस्याओं को नहीं समझते हैं।	1	2	3	4	5
7.	हमारे टीचर हमें करीब से जानते हैं।	1	2	3	4	5
8.	टीचर कमजोर स्टूडेन्ट्स पर कोई ध्यान नहीं देते।	1	2	3	4	5
9.	मेरा मन स्कूल से दूर रहने को करता है।	1	2	3	4	5
10.	बिना बात पर छात्रों को दंड (पनिशमेंट) दिया जाता है।	1	2	3	4	5
11.	मेरा स्कूल दूसरे स्कूलों से बहुत अच्छा है।	1	2	3	4	5
12.	मेरे स्कूल के नियम-कानून सख़्त हैं।	1	2	3	4	5
13.	मेरे स्कूल के टीचर बहुत अच्छे हैं।	1	2	3	4	5

	बहुत कम	कम	न कम न ज़्यादा	ज़्यादा	बहुत ज़्यादा
14. टीचर क्लास में सवाल पूछा जाना पसन्द नहीं करते।	1	2	3	4	5
15. सभी स्टूडेन्ट्स के लिए अनुशासन के नियम एक समान हैं।	1	2	3	4	5
16. टीचर हमारा मनोबल (कॉन्फिडेंस) बढ़ाते हैं।	1	2	3	4	5
17. टीचर कुछ बच्चों की तरफदारी करते हैं।	1	2	3	4	5
18. टीचर हमारे काम की तारीफ करते हैं।	1	2	3	4	5
19. क्लास की पढ़ाई अच्छी लगती है।	1	2	3	4	5

अब आपके अपने स्कूल के बारे में (हिन्दी या अंग्रेजी में लिखिए):

वे तीन बातें लिखिए जो आप अपने स्कूल के बारे में सबसे ज्यादा पसन्द (लाइक) करते हैं।

1. ______________________________

2. ______________________________

3. ______________________________

स्कूल से संबन्धित कौन सी तीन ऐसी बातें हैं, जिनको आप बदलना चाहेंगे।

1. ______________________________

2. ______________________________

3. ______________________________

भाग-2

अब आपसे पढ़ाई के बारे में कुछ बाते नीचे पूछी जा रही हैं। उत्तर देने का तरीका भाग-1 के समान ही है। बताइए आपके लिए ये बातें कितनी सही हैं?

		बहुत कम	कम	न कम न ज़्यादा	ज़्यादा	बहुत ज़्यादा
1.	मैं अपनी क्लास में अच्छी पोजीशन लाना चाहता हूँ।	1	2	3	4	5
2.	पढ़ाई मुझे बोझ लगती है।	1	2	3	4	5
3.	मैं चाहता हूँ कि किसी भी विषय में मेरा ज्ञान (नॉलेज) कम कच्चा न हो।	1	2	3	4	5
4.	किताबें पढ़ना मुझे अच्छा नहीं लगता।	1	2	3	4	5
5.	जिस दिन मैं नहीं पढ़ता, मुझे बहुत अच्छा लगता है।	1	2	3	4	5
6.	मैं अक्सर अपने साथियों से पढ़ाई के बारे में बात करता हूँ।	1	2	3	4	5
7.	मैं बहुत देर तक मन लगाकर नहीं पढ़ पाता।	1	2	3	4	5
8.	पढ़ते समय अगर मुझे कोई दूसरा काम करने के लिए कहे, तो मुझे अच्छा नहीं लगता।	1	2	3	4	5
9.	पता नहीं कब पढ़ाई से मेरी जान छूटेगी।	1	2	3	4	5
10.	जिस विषय (सब्जेक्ट) में मेरे कम नम्बर आते हैं, उसमें अधिक मेहनत नहीं करता हूँ।	1	2	3	4	5
11.	मुझे पढ़ने के लिए किसी को कहने की जरूरत नहीं पड़ती।	1	2	3	4	5
12.	मुश्किल सवालों को मैं चैलेंज की तरह लेता हूँ।	1	2	3	4	5

भाग-3

हम लोग एक दूसरे से बहुत बातों में फरक या अलग होते हैं। एक ही घटना पर लोगों का अलग-अलग व्यवहार (या रिएक्शन) होते हैं। आप अपने बारे में सोचें और यह बताएँ कि कहाँ तक नीचे किए गए व्यवहार (रिएक्शन) आपके मिज़ाज़ से मिलते हैं। हर व्यवहार को पढ़िए और सामने दिए गए उत्तरों, पूरा सच, आधा सच, पूरा झूठ, में से जो आपके लिए सही बैठे उस पर सही (√) का निशान लगाएँ।

		पूरा सच	आधा सच	पूरा झूठ
1.	ज़रा सी बात में खुश होना	1	2	3
2.	ज़रा सी बात में गुस्सा हो जाना	1	2	3
3.	ज़िद पकड़ लेना	1	2	3
4.	समझाने पर मान जाना	1	2	3
5.	नाराज़ होने पर अपने होशो हवास खो देनां	1	2	3
6.	खुशी की बात पर जरूरत से ज़्यादा ही खुश होना	1	2	3
7.	किसी का दुख देखकर खुद परेशान हो जाना	1	2	3
8.	किसी का छोटा सा भी दुख देखकर परेशान होना	1	2	3
9.	किसी दुख भरे सीन को देखने पर आँसू आ जाना	1	2	3
10.	किसी की कड़वी बात का मुंहतोड़ जवाब देना	1	2	3
11.	अपने मन की बात दूसरों को आसानी से बता न पाना।	1	2	3
12.	दूसरों की गलती पर डाँट पड़ने पर महसूस करना कि मुझे डाँटा जा रहा है।	1	2	3
13.	बिना सोचे समझे भी बोल देना।	1	2	3
14.	इस बात से परेशान रहना कि लोग मेरे बारे में क्या सोचते हैं।	1	2	3
15.	दूसरों के मुकाबले अपने बारे में ही सोचना।	1	2	3
16.	मदद की ज़रूरत होने पर भी न माँग पाना।	1	2	3
17.	दूसरों के जीतने पर उनसे जलन महसूस करना।	1	2	3
18.	थोड़ी देर के लिए नाराज़ हो ज़ाना पर फिर बिल्कुल नॉर्मल हो जाना।	1	2	3
19.	किसी बात को बहुत देर तक दिल में रखना।	1	2	3
20.	परिस्थिति (सिचुएशन) को देखकर व्यवहार करना।	1	2	3

2.1 किसी ऐसी घटना के बारे में सोचें जिसके मिलने पर आपको बहुत खुशी मिली हो।

(i) यह घटना क्या थी? ______________________

(ii) आपकी घटना के प्रति क्या प्रतिक्रिया (रिएक्शन) थी?

____

____

____

2.2 इसी प्रकार किसी ऐसी खबर के बारे में सोचे जिसके मिलने पर आपको दुख हुआ हो।

(i) यह घटना क्या थी?

____

____

____

(ii) घटना पर आपकी क्या प्रतिक्रिया रिसपौंस हुई?

____

____

____

भाग–4

एक छात्र होने के नाते आप अपने में कौन सी विशेषताएँ देखते हैं?

नीचे कुछ विशेषताएँ दी गई हैं। हर विशेषता के दो पहलू ही हैं। विशेषता का जो पहलू आप पर लागू होता है, उस पर गोले का निशान लगाएँ।

1. आलसी .... मेहनती
2. पढ़ाई चोर .... पढ़ाकू
3. बिना प्लान के काम करने वाला .... प्लान से काम करने वाला
4. पढ़ाई में कम तेज .... पढ़ाई में तेज
5. पढ़ाई में कम सफल .... पढ़ाई में सफल
6. देर से समझने वाला .... जल्दी समझने वाला
7. जल्दी भूलने वाला .... देर तक याद रखने वाला
8. घबरा जाने वाला .... आत्म विश्वासी
9. अपने को औरों के मुकाबले कम (इन्फीरियर) समझने वाला .... औरों के मुकाबले अपने को बेहतर (सुपीरियर) समझने वाला

10. गणित में कमजोर .... गणित में तेज

11. अन्य कोई ______________________

अब नीचे लिखे कथनों के उत्तर दें।

अपने साथियों के मुकाबले मेरी योग्यता है:

दूसरों से काफी कम	दूसरों से कम	दूसरों जैसी	दूसरों से ज्यादा	दूसरों से काफी ज़्यादा
1	2	3	4	5

अपने साथियों के मुकाबले, क्लास में मेरा काम (परफॉर्मेंस) है:

दूसरों से काफी कम	दूसरों से कम	दूसरों जैसी	दूसरों से ज़्यादा	दूसरों से काफी ज़्यादा
1	2	3	4	5

भाग-5

नीचे आपसे, आपके स्कूल और पढ़ने लिखने से सम्बन्धित आपकी परेशानियों के बारे में पूछा जा रहा है। दूसरे भागों की तरह हर बात पढ़िए और सही नम्बर को गोलकर के बताइए कि हर बात आपके लिए कितनी सही है।

		बहुत कम	कम	न कम न ज़्यादा	ज़्यादा	बहुत ज़्यादा
1.	परीक्षा का ख्याल मुझे डरा देता है।	1	2	3	4	5
2.	मुझे डर रहता है कि क्लास में कहीं मेरी हँसी न उड़े।	1	2	3	4	5
3.	क्योंकि मेरे माता-पिता मुझसे मेरी योग्यता से अधिक रिजल्ट की उम्मीद करते हैं, इसलिए मुझे परेशानी होती है।	1	2	3	4	5
4.	मुझे डर लगता है कि मैं इम्तहान में अच्छे नम्बर नहीं पा सकूँगा।	1	2	3	4	5
5.	मुझे अपने टीचरों से डर लगता है।	1	2	3	4	5
6.	मुझे अपने साथियों से बात करने में परेशानी होती है।	1	2	3	4	5
7.	मुझे डर लगता है कि मैं इम्तहान में अपने साथियों के मुकाबले अच्छा नहीं कर सकूँगा।	1	2	3	4	5
8.	मुझे डर है कि दूसरों के सामने मुझे कहीं लज्जित न होना पड़े।	1	2	3	4	5

भाग-6

अब आपसे व्यवसाय (कैरियर) के बारे में कुछ प्रश्न पूछे जा रहे हैं। उत्तर देने का तरीका पिछले भाग की तरह ही है। यह कहाँ तक सच है कि:

		बहुत कम	कम	न कम न ज़्यादा	ज़्यादा	बहुत ज़्यादा
1.	मुझे पता नहीं है, कि मैं पढ़ाई खत्म करने के बाद क्या करूँगा।	1	2	3	4	5
2.	मैं किस नौकरी, व्यवसाय में जाऊँ, इस बारे में मुझे कोई सलाह नहीं मिल रही है।	1	2	3	4	5
3.	मेरे माता-पिता जो मेरे लिए नौकरी, व्यवसाय चाह रहे हैं, यह मुझे पसन्द नहीं।	1	2	3	4	5
4.	मुझे लगता है कि जो मैं पढ़ रहा हूँ, उससे मुझे अच्छी नौकरी मिल पाएगी।	1	2	3	4	5
5.	मैं इस बात से परेशान हूँ कि मुझे अपनी पसन्द की नौकरी मिलेगी।	1	2	3	4	5
6.	मेरे पास नौकरियों के बारे में पूरी-पूरी जानकारी नहीं है।	1	2	3	4	5

क्रम संख्या:

नाम : लड़का/लड़की :

क्लास : स्कूल का नाम :

APPENDIX–B

रिसर्च-प्रश्नावली

(माता-पिता-फ़ॉर्म)

मनोविज्ञान विभाग, इलाहाबाद विश्वविद्यालय एवं सीमैट, इलाहाबाद, जनवरी, 1997

आप जानना चाहेंगे कि इस रिसर्च के द्वारा हम क्या पता लगाना चाहते हैं। हमारा मानना है कि ज्यादातर स्टूडेन्ट्स अपनी बुद्धि या क्षमता (इंटैलिजेंस) का पूरा-पूरा प्रयोग नहीं कर पाते हैं। जिसकी वजह से इम्तहानों में वे अपनी आशा और क्षमता से कम अच्छा करते हैं। आप से ली गयी जानकारी के आधार पर इन कारणों का पता लगा पाएँगे और हम विद्यार्थियों की बेहतर मदद कर पाएँगे।

आपके सहयोग के लिए धन्यवाद ।

अपने बेटे/बेटी   में आप कौन सी विशेषताएँ देखते हैं। नीचे कुछ विशेषताएँ दी गई हैं। हर विशेषता के दो पहलू होते हैं। हर विशेषता का जो पहलू आपके बेटे/बेटी के लिए सही हो, उस पर सही (√) का निशान लगाये।

1. आलसी ——— मेहनती
2. पढ़ाई चोर ——— पढ़ाकू
3. बिना प्लान के काम करने वाला ——— प्लान से काम करने वाला
4. पढ़ाई में कम तेज ——— पढ़ाई में तेज
5. पढ़ाई में कम सफल ——— पढ़ाई में सफल
6. देर से समझने वाला ——— जल्दी समझने वाला
7. जल्दी भूलने वाला ——— देर तक याद रखने वाला
8. घबरा जाने वाला ——— आत्मविश्वासी

9. अपने को औरों के मुकाबले कम (इन्फीरियर) समझने वाला	———	औरों के मुकाबले अपने को बेहतर (सुपीरियर)समझने वाला
10. गणित में कमजोर	———	गणित में तेज

अब आप अपने बेटे-बेटी की योग्यता परफॉर्मेंस के बारे में क्या सोचते हैं कृपया किसी एक पर सही (√) का निशान लगायें:

मेरे अनुसार क्लास के अन्य स्टूडेन्ट्स के मुकाबले, मेरे बेटे-बेटी की क्षमता/योग्यता है:

दूसरों से काफी कम	दूसरों से कम	दूसरों जैसी	दूसरों से ज्यादा	दूसरों से काफी ज़्यादा
1	2	3	4	5

अपने क्लास के अन्य स्टूडेन्ट्स के मुकाबले, मेरे बेटे-बेटी का परीक्षा में (परफॉर्मेंस)

दूसरों से काफ़ी खराब है	दूसरों से खराब है	दूसरों जैसी है	दूसरों से बेहतर है	दूसरों से काफ़ी बेहतर है
1	2	3	4	5

अपनी योग्यता या क्षमता की तुलना में मेरे बेटे-बेटी का (परफॉर्मेंस)

योग्यता से काफ़ी ज़्यादा अच्छा है	योग्यता से ज़्यादा अच्छा है	योग्यता के अनुसार ही है	योग्यता से कम अच्छा है	दूसरों से काफ़ी कम अच्छा है
1	2	3	4	5

कहा जाता है कि बच्चों की बहुत सी ऐसी समस्याएँ हैं जिनको ठीक से समझ नहीं पाते और मदद नहीं कर पाते हैं। अपने बच्चों की समस्याओं को सुलझाने के बारे में आप क्या सोचते हैं? नीचे कुछ कथन/प्रश्न दिये गए हैं। हर कथन के सामने 3 अंक दिये गए हैं। जैसे:

कम जरूरी	जरूरी	अधिक जरूरी
1	2	3

यदि आपको यह कथन कम जरूरी लगता है तो 1 को गोले से घेर दें, अगर जरूरी लगता है तो 2 और अगर अधिक जरूरी लगता है तो 3 को गोले से घेर दें:

आपको लगता है कि स्कूल में कोई ऐसा व्यक्ति (सलाहकार) होना चाहिए, जिससे:

		कम जरूरी	जरूरी	अधिक जरूरी
1.	बच्चे अपनी परेशानियों के बारे में बात कर सकें।	1	2	3
2.	जो बच्चे की पढ़ाई की दिक्कतों को दूर करने में मदद करें।	1	2	3
3.	जो बच्चे की बुद्धि (इंटेलिजेंस) को नापे।	1	2	3
4.	बच्चे की विशेष योग्यताओं (टैलेन्ट) को पहचानने में मदद कर सके।	1	2	3
5.	बच्चे की योग्यता के अनुसार विषय चुनने में मदद कर सके।	1	2	3
6.	भविष्य के व्यवसायों के बारे में जानकारी और सलाह दे।	1	2	3
7.	पढ़ने की आदतों को बेहतर बनाने में बच्चों की मदद कर सके।	1	2	3
8.	बच्चे के बेहतर विकास के लिए माता-पिता को सलाह दे।	1	2	3
9.	क्लास के माहौल को बेहतर बनाने में टीचर की मदद कर सके।	1	2	3
10.	पढ़ाई को रोचक (इंटेरेस्टिंग) बनाने में सहायता कर सके।	1	2	3
11.	बच्चे को व्यवसाय चुनने के लिए रास्ता दिखा सके।	1	2	3
12.	बच्चों को माता-पिता किस तरह संभाले (ढालें), इस बारे में सलाह दे सके।	1	2	3
13.	हमको बच्चों की विशेष योग्यताओं को उभारने के तरीके बता सके।	1	2	3

14. बड़े होने पर आप अपने बच्चे को क्या बनाना चाहेंगे?

(सबसे अधिक चाहने वाले को पहले लिखें, फिर उसके बाद दूसरे, तीसरे और चौथे नंबर वाले व्यवसायों को)

1. ______________________________

2. ______________________________

3. ______________________________

4. ______________________________

15. जिस नौकरी/व्यवसाय में आप अपने बच्चे को सबसे अधिक भेजना चाहते हैं, उसमें उसके चले जाने की कितनी संभावना है?

थोड़ी कम संभावना है	बीच की संभावना है	पूरी संभावना है
1	2	3

यदि इस व्यवसाय में आपका बच्चा चला गया तो सब कुछ देखते हुए इस व्यवसाय/नौकरी में वह कहाँ तक सफल होगा?

कुछ सफल	औसत सफल	बहुत सफल
1	2	3

बच्चे का नाम : कक्षा :

माता/पिता का नाम :

स्कूल का नाम : पिता की शिक्षा :

व्यवसाय :

माँ की शिक्षा : व्यवसाय :

घर की अंदाजन मासिक आय :

क्या बच्चे के पास पढ़ने के लिए अपनी जगहे है? हाँ/नहीं

क्या बच्चे को जिन पुस्तकों की जरूरत है वह उसके पास है? सभी/ज्यादातर/कम ही

क्या बच्चा केवल अपने आप पढ़ता है? हाँ/नहीं

यदि उसे कोई पढ़ाता है तो कौन

घर का ही कोई व्यक्ति

मास्टर/ट्यूशन

आपके बच्चे की कौन सी समस्या है जिससे आप को चिंता होती है?

प्रश्नकर्ता का नाम

APPENDIX–C

रिसर्च-प्रश्नावली

(टीचर-फ़ॉर्म)

मनोविज्ञान विभाग, इलाहाबाद विश्वविद्यालय एवं सीमैट, इलाहाबाद, जनवरी, 1997

आप जानना चाहेंगे कि इस रिसर्च के द्वारा हम क्या पता लगाना चाहते हैं। हमारा मानना है कि ज्यादातर स्टूडेन्ट्स अपनी क्षमता या बुद्धि (इंटैलिजैंस) का पूरा-पूरा प्रयोग नहीं कर पाते हैं जिसकी वजह से इम्तहानों में वे अपनी आशा और क्षमता से कम अच्छा करते हैं। आपसे ली गई जानकारी के आधार पर हम ऐसे कारणों का पता पाएँगे और विद्यार्थियों की बेहतर मद्द कर पाएँगे। इस फॉर्म में आपके स्टूडेन्ट सम्बन्धी और उनकी प्रॉब्लम (समस्या) से सम्बन्धी प्रश्न हैं।

आपके सहयोग के लिए धन्यवाद।

आपके स्कूल का नाम ____________________

किस क्लास में क्लास टीचर हैं? ____________________

इस क्लास को कौन सा विषय पढ़ाते हैं? ____________________

आप कितने सालों से पढ़ा रहे हैं? ____________________

आपका नाम ____________________

एक टीचर होने के नाते आप अपने स्टूडेन्ट____________ में कौन सी विशेषताएँ देखते हैं। नीचे कुछ विशेषताएँ दी गई हैं। हर विशेषता के दो पहलू होते हैं। हर विशेषता का जो पहलू इस स्टूडेन्ट पर लागू होता है, उस पर सही (√) का निशान लगाएँ।

1.	आलसी	———	मेहनती
2.	पढ़ाई चोर		पढ़ाकू
3.	बिना प्लान के काम करने वाला	———	प्लान से काम करने वाला
4.	पढ़ाई में कम तेज	———	पढ़ाई में तेज
5.	पढ़ाई में कम सफल	———	पढ़ाई में सफल
6.	देर से समझने वाला	———	जल्दी समझने वाला
7.	जल्दी भूलने वाला	———	देर तक याद रखने वाला
8.	घबरा जाने वाला	———	आत्मविश्वासी
9.	अपने को औरों के मुकाबले कम (इन्फीरियर) समझने वाला	———	औरों के मुकाबले अपने को बेहतर (सुपीरियर) समझने वाला
10.	गणित में कमजोर	———	गणित में तेज

हम अब आपसे इस छात्र की योग्यता/परफॉर्मेंस के बारे में पूछना चाहेंगे। कृपया किसी एक पर सही (√) का निशान लगायें :

अपने क्लास के अन्य स्टूडेन्ट्स के मुकाबले आपके इस स्टूडेन्ट की योग्यता, या क्षमता है।

दूसरों से काफ़ी खराब है	दूसरों से खराब है	दूसरों जैसी है	दूसरों से बेहतर है	दूसरों से काफ़ी बेहतर है
1	2	3	4	5

अपने क्लास के अन्य स्टूडेन्ट्स के मुकाबले आपके इस स्टूडेन्ट्स की परीक्षा में परफॉर्मेंस।

काफ़ी ख़राब	ख़राब	औसत	अच्छी	काफ़ी अच्छी
1	2	3	4	5

अपनी योग्यता या क्षमता की तुलना में इसकी परफॉर्मेंस।

योग्यता से काफ़ी नीचे	योग्यता से नीचे	योग्यता से बराबर	योग्यता से अच्छी	योग्यता से काफ़ी अच्छी
1	2	3	4	5

रिकार्ड से शोध–सहायक के भरने के लिए

छमाही (हाफ इयरली) परीक्षा में बच्चे के नम्बर (टोटल मार्कस)

प्रतिशत (ओवर ऑल परसन्टेज) ______________________

गणित के नम्बर (मार्कस) ______________________

गणित के प्रतिशत (परसन्टेज) ______________________

पिछली क्लास का रिकॉर्ड ______________________

प्राप्त नम्बर (टोटल मार्कस) ______________________

प्रतिशत (ओवरऑल परसन्टेज) ______________________

गणित के नम्बर (मार्कस) ______________________

गणित के प्रतिशत (परसन्टेज) ______________________

BIBLIOGRAPHY

Agarwal, S.K. (1977). A psychological study of academic underachievement. *Indian Educational Review, 12,* 105-110.

Akhani, P., Rathi, N., & Josore, M. (1999). Academic habits and loneliness of children of employed and unemployed mothers. *Indian Journal of Psychometry and Education*, *30,* 65-67.

Ames, C. (1987). The enhancement of student motivation. In *Advances in motivation and achievement: Enhancing motivation* (Vol.5, pp.123-148). Greewich, CT:JAI Press.

Ames, C. (1992). Achievement goals and the classroom motivational climate. In D.H. Schunk & J.L. Meece (Eds.), *Student perceptions in the classroom* (pp.327-348). Hillsdale, NJ: Erlbaum.

Ames, C., & Archer, J. (1988). Achievement goals in the classroom: Student's learning strategies and motivation processes. *Journal of Educational Psychology, 80*, 260-267.

Anastasi, A. (1979). *Field of applied psychology.* (Second edition). New York: McGraw–Hill.

Angira, K.K. (1994). Effect of family structure and gender on achievement motivation. *Purvanchal Journal of Social Sciences,* 2, 34-38.

Baker, S.B. *School counselling for the twenty-first century.* (Second edition) Englewood Cliffs: Prentice-Hall.

Bajpai, N. & Goyal, S. (2004). Primary education in India: Quality and coverage issues. CGSD Working Paper No. 11. (www.earthinstitute.columbia.edu/cgsd/documents)

Basantia, J. & Mukhopadhyaya, D. (2001). Effect of environmental factors on achievement: A study of rural school students. *The Educational Review, 44,* 301-304.

Baumrind, D. (1971). Current patterns of parental authority. *Developmental Psychology Monographs, 4,* 1-102.

Baumrind, D. (1973). The development of instrumental competence through socialization. In A.D. Pick (Ed.) *Minnesota Symposium of Child Psychology VII.* Minneapolis: Univ. of Minnesota Press.

Bessell, H., & Palamares, U. (1969). *Human development program.* San Diego, Ca: Human Development Training Institute, Inc.

Bissa, S., Singh, B.G., & Verma, O.P. (1992). Academic achievement: A insecurity feelings. *Perspectives in Psychological Researchers, 15(1),* 11-15.

Boekarts, M. (1993). Being concerned with well-being and with learning. *Educational Psychologist, 28,* 149-167.

Borkowski, J.G., & Thorpe, P.K. (1994). Self-regulation and motivation: A life-span perspective on underachievement. In D.H. Schunk & B.J. Zimmerman (Eds.), *Self-regulation of learning and performance: Issues and educational applications* (pp.45-74). Hillsdale, NJ: Erlbaum.

Brookover, W.B. (1978). Elementary school social climate and school achievement. *American Educational Research Journal, 15,* 301-318.

Brophy, J.E. (1979). Teacher behaviour and its effects. *Journal of Educational Psychology, 71,* 733-750.

Brophy, J.E., & Good, T.E. (1974). *Teacher-student relationships: Causes and consequences.* New York: Holt, Rinehart & Winston.

Buch, M.B. (1972). Educational psychology: A trend report. In S.K. Mitra (Ed.) *A survey of research in psychology.* Bombay: Popular Prakashan.

Buck, M.R., & Austrin, H.R. (1971). Factors related to school achievement in an economically disadvantaged group. *Child Development, 42,* 1813-1825.

Chandra, P. (1994). Goal setting behaviour and achievement. *Osmania Journal of Psychology, 17,* 1-8.

Chandra, P. (1994-95). Modelling and goal setting behaviour. *Osmania Journal of Psychology, 19,* 49-56.

Chandra, P. (1995). Goal setting behaviour and reward. *Journal of Psychology, 20,* 52-58.

Chatterjee, B.B. (1977). Pattern of school achievement in primary grades. *Indian Educational Review, 12,* 29-67.

Chauhan, V., & Murthy, S. (1994). Effect of achievement on adjustment of deprived adolescents. *Psycho-Lingua, 24 (1),* 49-53.

Chinnian, R.R., & Iyengar, M.S. (1984).Psychometric correlates of scholastic performance. *Indian Journal of Clinical Psychology, 11,* 1-8.

Contractor, B.M. (1976). Role of intelligence, extraversion and neuroticism in three examination results. In A. Shah (Ed.) *A comprehensive research report.* Ahmedabad: Behavioural Research Publication.

Cooper, H.M. (1979). Pygmalion grows up: A model for teacher expectation communication and performance influence. *Review of Educational Research, 49,* 389-410.

Covington, M.V. (2000). Goal theory, motivation and school achievement: An integrative review. *Annual Review of Psychology, 51,* 171-200.

Crandall, V.C. (1969). Sex differences in expectancy of intellectual and academic reinforcement. In C.P. Smith (Ed.) *Achievement related motives in children.* New York: Russell Sage.

Daftuar, C.N., Sinha, C. & Daftuar, L. (2000). Academic achievement and risk-taking among tribal and non-tribal students of rural and urban area. *Psychological Studies, 45,* 103-105.

Davids, A., & Hainsworth, P.K. (1967). Maternal attitudes about family life and child rearing as avowed by mothers and perceived by their underachieving and high-achieving sons. *Journal of Consulting Psychology, 31,* 29-37.

Deci, E., & Ryan, R. (1985). *Intrinsic motivation and self-determination in human behaviour.* New York: Academic Press.

Dekhtawala, P.B. (1978). *A study of organizational climate, leadership behaviour, teacher morale and pupils' academic motivation in secondary schools of Gujarat state.* Research Report, Centre of Advanced Study in Education, M.S. University, Baroda.

Devi, M.S., & Kiran, K. (2002). Family factors associated with scholastic backwardness of secondary school children. *Journal of Community Guidance and Research, 19,* 167-172.

Dishion, T.J., French, D.C., & Patterson, G.R. (1995). The development and ecology of antisocial behaviour. In D.Cicchetti & D.J. Cohen (Eds.), *Developmental Psychopathology: Volume 2. Risk, disorder, and adaptation* (pp. 421-471). New York: Wiley.

Dreze, J. & Sen, A. (2002). *Indian development and participation.* New Delhi: Oxford University Press.

Dryfoos, J.G. (1994). *Adolescents at risk: Prevalence and Prevention.* New York: Oxford University Press.

Dubey, R.S. (1976). Manifest anxiety & educational performance. *Psychological Studies, 21,* 52-58.

Dudek, S.Z., & Lester, E.P. (1968). The good child façade in chronic underachievers. *American Journal of Orthopsychiarty, 38,* 153-160.

Durlak, J.A. (1995). *School-based prevention programs for children and adolescents.* Thousand Oaks, CA: Sage.

Dweck, C.S. & Elliott, E.S. (1983). Achievement motivation (pp. 643-693). In E. Mavis Hetherington (Vol.Ed.) Socialization, personality and social development (Vol. IV). In P.H. Mussen (Ed.), *Handbook of child psychology,* New York: John Wiley.

Dweck, C.S., & Leggett, E. (1988). A social-cognitive approach to motivation and personality. *Psychological Review, 95*, 256-273.

Dweck, C.S., & Wortman, C.B. (1982). Learned helplessness, anxiety, and achievement motivation: Neglected parallels in cognitive, affective, and coping responses. In H. Kronhe & L. Laux (Eds.), *Achievement, stress, and anxiety* (pp.93-125). Washington, DC: Hemisphere.

Eccles, J.S. (1983). Expectancies, values and academic behaviours. In J.T. Spence (Ed.), *The development of achievement motivation* (pp. 283-331). Greenwich, CT:JAI Press.

Eccles, J.S., Lord, S., & Roeser, R.W. (1996). Round holes, square pegs, rocky roads, and sore feet: A discussion of stage-environment fit theory applied to families and schools. In D. Cicchetti & S.L. Toth (Eds.) *Rochester Symposium on Developmental Psychopathologies: Volume VII. Adolescence: Opportunities and Challenges* (pp. 47-92). Rochester, NY: University of Rochester Press.

Eccles, J.S., Midgley, C., & Adler, T. (1984). Grade-related changes in the school environment: Effects on achievement motivation. In J. Nicholls (Ed.), *Advances in motivation and achievement* (Vol.3, pp. 283-331). Greenwich, CT: JAI Press.

Eccles, J.S., Wigfield, A., & Schiefele, U. (1998). Motivation to succeed. In W. Damon (Ed.), N. Eisenberg (Series Ed.), *Handbook of child psychology: Vol. 3. Social, emotional, and personality development* (5th ed., pp.1017-1095). New York: Wiley.

Eisner, F. (1994). *Cognition and curriculum reconsidered.* New York: Teacher's College Press.

Feuerstein, R. (1982). *Instrumental enrichment.* Baltimore: University Press.

Fine, M. (1991). *Framing dropouts: Notes on the politics of an urban public high school.* Albany: State University of New York. Press.

Ganguli, P.K. (1983). Anxiety and academic achievement. *Journal of Educational Research & Extension, 19,* 233-238.

Gardner, H. (1993). *Frames of mind: The theory of multiple intelligences.* London: Fontana.

Garg, K. (1981). Self-esteem and academic achievement among adolescents. *Progress of Education, 55,* 156-159.

Goleman, D. (1995). *Emotional intelligence.* New York: Bantam.

Goleman, D. (1998). *Working with emotional intelligence.* New York: Bantam.

Good, T.L. (1980). *Teacher expectations, teacher behaviour, student perceptions and student behaviour: A decade of research,* Paper presented at the meetings of the American Educational Research Association.

Goodenow, C. (1993). Classroom belonging among early adolescent students: Relationships to motivation and achievement. *Journal of Early Adolescence, 13,* 21-43.

Gotlib, I.H., & MacLeod, C. (1997). Information processing in anxiety and depression: A cognitive-developmental perspective. In J.A. Burack & J.T. Enns (Eds.), *Attention, development, and psychopathology* (pp.350-378). New York: Guilford Press.

Graham, S. (1997). Using attribution theory to understand social and academic motivation in African American Youth. *Educational Psychologist, 32,* 21-34.

Gupta, A.K., & Sharma, S.K. (1987). *Parental influences on adolescents.* New Delhi: Ariana Publishing House.

Gupta, R. (2000). Prolonged deprivation and attainment of students. *Psychological Studies, 45,* 96-99.

Hermans, H.J., Ter-Laak, J.J. & Maes, P.C. (1972). Achievement motivation and fear of failure in family and school. *Developmental Psychology, 6,* 520-528.

Hinshaw, S.P. (1992). Externalizing behaviour problems and academic underachievement in childhood and adolescence: Causal relationships and underlying mechanisms. *Psychological Bulletin, 111,* 127-155.

Holland, J.L. & Holland J.E. (1977). Vocational indecision: More evidence and speculation. *Journal of Counselling Psychology, 24,* 404-414.

Honig, A.S. (Ed., 1990). *Early parenting and later child achievement.* New York: Gordon & Breach Science Publishers.

Hummell, R., & Sprinthall, N. (1965). Underachievement related to interests, attitudes, and values. *Personnel and Guidance Journal, 44,* 388-395.

Institute of Medicine (1994). *Reducing risks for mental disorders: Frontiers for preventive intervention research.* Washington, DC: National Academy Press.

Jackson, Y. (2001). Reversing underachievement in urban students: Pedagogy of confidence. In A. Costa (Ed.) *Developing minds:*

A resource book for teaching thinking. Alexandria,VA: Association for Supervision and Curriculum Development. (www.nuatc.org/articles)

Jindal, C.R., & Panda, B.K. (1982). Anxiety and achievement: A research study of high & low achievers. *Indian Educational Review,17,* 118-124.

Kakkar, S.K. (1977). Intelligence, curiosity and achievement. *ISPT Journal of Research, 1,* 131-136.

Kakkar, S.K., & Wali, S.K. (1978). Creatively and intelligence as predictions of academic achievement. *Social Science Research Journal, 3,* 83-96.

Kapur, M. (1997). *Mental health in Indian schools.* New Delhi: Sage.

Katyal, S., & Vasudeva, P. (2001). Gender differences in academic stress and its correlates. *Personality Study and Group Behaviour, 21,* 31-38.

Kaur, B. (1994). *Extent and quality of home and school support for children's academic success.* Paper presented at the sixth international round table on Families, Communities, Schools and Children's Learning. Institute of Responsive Education, New Orleans.

Kaur, B., Menon, S., & Konantambigi, R. (2001). Child and adolescent development research. In J. Pandey (Ed.) *Psychology in India revisited—Developments in the discipline.* Vol. 2: Personality and Health Psychology (pp.163-227). New Delhi: Sage.

Kessler, R.C., Foster, C.L., Saunders, W.B., & Stang P.E. (1995). Social consequences of psychiatric disorders: Educational attainment. *American Journal of Psychiatry, 152,* 102-111.

Kiranmayi, A., & Vindhya, U. (1996). Field dependence–independence as a function of socio-economic status and academic achievement: A study on adolescent girls. *Journal of Indian Psychology, 14, (1&2),* 31-40.

Knitzer, J., Steinberg, Z., & Fleisch, B. (1991). Schools, children's mental health, and the advocacy challenge. *Journal of Clinical Child Psychology, 20,* 102-111.

Kohli, T., & Joshi, J.W. (1978). Behavioural and environment correlates of academic achievement and over and underachievement. *Social Science Research Journal, 3,* 41-52.

Kumar, K. (1975). Social climate in school and characteristics of pupils. *Indian Journal of Clinical Psychology, 2,* 162-172.

Kumaran, D.L. (2001). A study of organizational climate and academic performance of higher secondary schools. *The Educational Review, 44,* 3-7.

Lunneborg, P.W. (1975). Interest differentiation in high school & vocational indecision in college. *Journal of Vocational Behaviour, 7,* 297-303.

Maikhuri, R., & Panda, S.K. (1997). Self-concept of adolescents in relation to their academic achievement. *Psycho-Lingua, 27 (2),* 121-124.

Mathew, T. (1976). *Some personality factors related to underachievement in science.* Doctoral dissertation, University of Kerala, Trivendrum.

Maughan, B. (1988). School experiences as risk/protective factors. In M. Rutter (Ed.), *Studies of psychosocial risk: The power of longitudinal data* (pp. 200-220). New York: Cambridge University Press.

Mehdi, B. (1974). Creativity, intelligence and achievement. Some findings of recent research. *Indian Educational Review, 9,* 1-10.

MHRD (1994). Ministry of Human Resource Development, Government of India. (www.education.nic.in)

Midgley, C., Feldlaufer, H., Eccles, J.S. (1989b). Student/teacher relations and attitudes towards mathematics before and after the transition to junior high school. *Child Development, 90,* 981-992.

Miller, G.W. (1970). Factors in schools achievement and social class. *Journal of Educational psychology, 61,* 260-269.

Minuchin, P.P., & Shapiro, E.K. (1983). The school as a context for social development (pp. 197-274). In E. Mavis Hetherington (Vol.Ed.) Socialization, personality and social development (Vol. IV) In P.H. Mussen (Ed.) *Handbook of child psychology*. New York: John Wiley.

Mishra, R.C. (2002). Cognitive self and its development in different quality of schools. *Journal of Indian Psychology, 20,* 1-10.

Mishra, R.C., & Agarwal, A. (2002). Perceptual differentiation in Hindu and Muslim children of traditional and modern schools. *Social Science International, 18,* 16-25.

Misra, G. (1983). Deprivation and development: A review of Indian studies. *Indian Educational Review, 18,* 12-22.

Mohanty, N. (2000). School type, psychological differentiation and academic achievement of tribal and non-tribal children. *Psychological Studies, 45,* 100-102.

Moos, R.H. (1979). *Evaluating educational environments.* San Francisco: Jossey-Bass.

Morrow, W.R. (1970). Academic underachievement. In C.G. Costello (Ed.) *Symptoms of psychopathology.* New York: Wiley.

Mukerjee, R., & Nayar, P. (1995). A comparative study of the test scores of above and below normal school students for intelligence and aggression. *Journal of Applied Psychological Issues, 1,* 33-35.

Murthy, M.S.R. (1980). A study into the effect of impulsiveness and controlledness over academic achievement. *Indian Educational Review, 15,* 103-114.

Nair, A.S. (1981). Some social familial variables causing underachievement in secondary school mathematics. *Journal of Educational Research and Extension, 18,* 10-14.

Nicholls, J.G. (1984). Achievement motivation: Conceptions of ability, subjective experience, task choice, and performance. *Psychological Review, 91,* 328-346.

Nolen-Hoeksma, S., Girgus, J.S., & Seligman, M.E.P. (1986). Learned helplessness in children: A longitudinal study of depression, achievement, and explanatory style. *Journal of Personality and Social Psychology, 51,* 435-442.

Padhi, J., & Dash, A.S. (1994). Thc relation of parental attitudes to adolescent competence. *Psycho-Lingua, 24 (1),* 33-42.

Panda, B.N., Sahoo, K.D., & Sahoo, J. (1995). Influence of school organisational climate on students' academic achievement. *Indian Journal of Applied Psychology, 32 (1&2),* 34-39.

Panda, K.C. (1988). Social psychology of education. In J. Pandey (Ed.) *Psychology in India: The state of the art.* (Vol. 2, Basic and applied social psychology). New Delhi: Sage.

Pande, N. (1980). Irregular attendance at school: climate support for SC students. *Social Change, March-June,* 19-22.

Pande, N., & Tripathi, R.C. (1982). Scheduled caste children in high caste school: Some motivational consequences. In D. Sinha, R.C. Tripathi & G. Misra (Eds.) *Deprivation: Its social roots and psychological consequences.* New Delhi: Concept.

Parikh, B.A. (1976, 1977). Educational achievement in relation to socio-economic status, parental education and occupation. *Journal of Psychological and Educational Research, 2-3,* 7-12.

Phillips, B.N. (1983). School problems of adolescence. In C.E. Walker & M.C. Roberts (Ed.) *Handbook of clinical child psychology.* New York: John Wiley.

Pierce, J.V., & Bowman, P.H. (1960). *Motivation patterns of superior high school students: The gifted student.*

Pintrinch, P., & De Groot, E.V. (1990). Motivational and self-regulated learning components of classroom academic performance. *Journal of Educational Psychology, 82,* 33-40.

PROBE Team (1999). *Public report on basic education.* Oxford: Oxford University Press.

Rajamanickam, M., & Vasanthal, R. (1993). Adjustment problems of adolescent students in relation to their achievements. *Journal of Community Guidance and Research, 10 (2),* 153-183.

Ramachandran, K.M. (1993). *Social and familial variables which cause underachievement in Malayalam in secondary schools.* Ph.D. Education, University of Calicut.

Ramaswamy, R. (1989). Self-image and academic striving. *Experiments in Education, 17 (4),* 83-87.

Rangappa, K.T. (1994). Effect of self-concept on achievement in Maths. *Psycho-Lingua, 24 (1),* 24 (1), 43-48.

Rani, R., & Reddy, K.R. (1995). The relationship between the rate of learning and achievement motivation among high school boys. *Osmania Journal of Psychology,* 20, 26-30.

Rao, S.N. (1963). Students' performance in relation to certain aspects of personality and academic adjustment. Unpublished Ph.D. thesis. Tirupati: S.V. University.

Rao, S.N. (1964). A study of the sense of responsibility and its relation to academic achievement. *Psychological Studies, 9 (2),* (other details not available).

Rao, Y.R. (1976). *A study of the relationship of few selected variables on the academic achievement indices of secondary on schools.* Doctoral dissertation, University of Madras, Madras.

Rath, R., Dash, A.S., & Dash, U.N. (1979). *Cognitive abilities and school achievements of the socially disadvantaged children in primary schools.* Bombay: Allied Publishers.

Richer, S. (1974). Middle-class bias of schools: Fact or fancy. *Sociology of Education, 47,* 523-534.

Roeser, R.W., & Eccles, J.S. (2000). Schooling and mental health. In A.J. Sameroff, M. Lewis & S.M. Miller (Eds.) *Handbook of developmental psychopathology* (2nd ed., pp. 135-156). New York: Kluwer Academic/Plenum.

Roeser, R.W., Eccles, J.S., & Strobel, K. (1998). Linking the study of schooling and mental health: Selected issues and empirical illustrations at the level of the individual. *Educational Psychologist, 33,* 153-176.

Roeser, R.W., Midgley, C.M., & Urdan, T.C. (1996). Perceptions of the school psychological environment and early adolescents' psychological and behavioural functioning in school: The mediating role of goals and belonging. *Journal of Educational Psychology, 88,* 408-422.

Rogoff, B. (1990). *Apprenticeship in thinking: Cognitive environment in social context.* New York: Oxford University Press.

Rosenthal, R., Jacobson, L. (1968). *Pygmalion in the classroom: Teacher expectations and pupils' intellectual development.* New York: Holt, Rinehart & Winston.

Roth, R.M., & Puri, P. (1967). The direction of aggression and the

Non-Achievement Syndrome. *Journal of Counselling Psychology, 14,* 277-281.

Roy, G.S., Sinha, R.K., & Hassan, M. (1994). Impact of headship style upon social emotional climate, academic achievement and campus activities of students. *Journal of the Indian Academy of Applied Psychology, 20 (1),* 83-86.

Ryan, R.M., & Grolnick, W. (1986). Origins and pawns in the classroom: Self-report and projective assessments of individual differences in children's perceptions. *Journal of Personality and Social Psychology, 50,* 550-558.

Sabberwal, N.D. (1967). Emotional tension and its effect on students performance in school examination. *Education and Psychology Review,* (other details not available).

Salovey, P., & Mayer, J.D. (1990). Emotional Intelligence. *Imagination, Cognition & Personality, 9,* 185-211.

Salovey, P., & Mayer, J.D. (1990). Emotional intelligence. *Imagination, Cognition and Personality, 9,* 185-211.

Sameroff, A.J. (1987). The social context of development. In N. Eisenberg (Ed.) *Contemporary topics in developmental psychology.* (pp. 273-291). New York: Wiley.

Santhanam, R.M., & Sharma, M.L. (1972). Classroom interaction analysis and school organizational climate. *Progress of Education, 41,* 23-27.

Saraswat, R.K., & Gaur, J.S. (1979). The role of self-concept in academic achievement: review of Indian researchers. *ISPT Journal of Research, 3,* 35-38.

Sattler, H.E., & Van Wagener, K. (1975). Motivation as an outcome of schooling. *Perceptual & Motor Skills, 41,* 993-994.

Schaefer, C. (1997). Motivation: A major cause of underachievement. *Devereux Forum, 12,* 16-29.

Schultz, C.B., & Aurbach, H.A. (1971). The usefulness of cumulative deprivation as an explanation of educational deficiencies. *Merrill-Palmer Quarterly, 17,* 27-39.

Segal, Z.V., & Clooitre, M. (1993). Methodologies for studying cognitive features of emotional disorder. In K.S. Dobson & P.C. Kendall (Eds.), *Psychopathology and Cognition* (pp.19-50). San Diego: Academic Press.

Seligman, M.E.P., Peterson, C., Kaslow, N.J., Tanenbaum, R.L., Alloy, L.B., & Abramson, L.Y. (1984). Attributional style and depressive symptoms among children. *Journal of Abnormal Psychology, 93,* 235-238.

Seth, P. (1978). Low academic achievement and emotionality. *Indian Educational Review, 13,* 97-102.

Sharma, M., Mehta, M. (1993). The effects of discordance between interest and chosen curriculum upon psychological adjustment and academic achievement. *Indian Journal of Psychometry and Education, 24 (1),* 25-30.

Sharma, R. (1985). *Attribution of success and failure in school.* Unpublished doctoral dissertation, University of Allahabad, Allahabad.

Sharma, S. (1978). Anxiety and academic achievement: A review of research. *Indian Educational Review, 13,* 54-73.

Sharma, S., & Tripathi, H. (1982). A study of field dependence – independence in high school students as a function of sex, academic achievement, and rural urban habitation. *Personality and Group Behaviour, 2,* 11-14.

Shivappa, P. (1969). A study of the relationship between academic achievement and self-concept of high-school pupils. *Journal of the College of Education, 5 (2),* (other details not available).

Shivrathanma, N. (1981). Scholastic achievement in relation to academic motivation. *Indian Journal of Clinical psychology, 8,* 128-131.

Singh, S. (2000). To dispel fantasies about the fantasy-based measure of motive to avoid success: Another look. *Journal of Research and Application in Clinical Psychology,* 111, 33-40.

Singh, S., & Saxena, R.P. (1995). Achievement differences and school effects. *Indian Educational Review,* Special Issue, 1-25.

Sinha, D. (1980). Some cognitive and motivational concomitants of poverty. *Social Change, 10,* 3-8.

Sinha, D. (1982). Some social disadvantages and development of certain perceptual skills. In D. Sinha, R.C. Tripathi, & G.

Misra (Eds.) *Deprivation: Its social roots and psychological consequences.* New Delhi: Concept.

Shukla, P., & Sinha, D. (1974). A developmental study of the relative efficacy of different pictorial cues in depth perception. *Indian Journal of Psychology, 49,* 220-230.

Srivastava, A.K. (1961). Reading ability and underachievement. *Indian Educational Review, 4 (1),* (other details not available).

Srivastava, A.K. (1966). An investigation into the factors related to educational underachievement. Unpublished Ph.D. thesis: Patna University.

Srivastava, A.K. (1967). A critical examination of the different types of criterion variables used for identifying underachievers. *Patna University Journal, 22 (1),* (other details not available).

Srivastava, R.K. (1995). Effect of the parent-child relationship perception upon the academic achievement of Vth class pupils. *Praachi Journal of Psycho Cultural Dimensions, 11,* 27-31.

Srivastava, U., & Chandiramani, R. (1995). Scholastic achievement as a function of cognitive style and family environment. *Psycho-Lingua, 25 (1&2),* 61-64.

Stipek, D.J., & Hoffman, J.M. (1980). Children's achievement related expectancies as a function of academic performance histories and sex, *Journal of Educational Psychology, 72,* 861-865.

Subrahmanyam, S., & Ramadevi, M. (1991). Some differential characteristics of high and low achievers in secondary schools. *Experiments in Education, 19 (8),* 228-232.

Sundranjan, S., & Selviraj Gnanaguru, A. (1992). High school pupils' academic achievement motivation and their academic achievement. *Experiments in Education, 20 (6),* 158-164.

Teichmann, H., Gollnitz, G., & Gohler, I. (1975). The origin and effects on school children of high parental demands for achievement. *International Journal of Mental Health, 4,* 83-106.

Thapa, K. (1998). *Psychological contributions to quality education: The role and functions of school psychologists.* Paper presented at the Seminar on Quality Education, 2-3 Feb. 1998, Maharishi Patnajali Vidya Mandir, Allahabad.

Tripathi, R.C. (1988). Applied social psychology. In. J. Pandey (Ed.), *Psychology in India: The state of the art. Vol. 2: Basic and applied social psychology* (pp. 95-157). New Delhi: Sage.

Trivedi, R.M. (1995). Anxiety level and academic achievement of undergraduate students. *Experiments in Education, 23 (3),* 47-51.

UNICEF (2004). *The state of the world's children.* Geneva: UNICEF.

Urdan, T. (1997). Achievement goal theory: Past results, future directions. In P.R. Pintrinch & M.L. Maehr (Eds.), *Advances in motivation and achievement*, Vol. 10 (pp. 99-142). Greenwich, CN: JAI.

Urdan, T.C., & Maehr, M.L. (1995). Beyond a two-goal theory of motivation and achievement: A case for social goals. *Review of Educational Research, 65,* 213-243.

Venugopal, G. (1995).The influence of teacher attitude and expectations on pupils' achievement. *Experiments in Education, 23 (1),* 12-18.

Verhulst, F.C., & Koot, H.M. (1992). *Child psychiatric epidemiology: Concepts, methods and findings.* Newbury Park, CA: Sage.

Verma, N., & Sinha, S. (2000). Time orientation and academic achievement. *Journal of Psychological Issues, 8,* 59-64.

Verma, P., & Verma, S. (2000). A study of academic achievement in relation to intelligence, parental involvement and adolescent girls' motivational resources: A path analytic study of mothers' and fathers' contribution. *Personality Study and Group Behaviour,* 59-82.

Verma, S. & Kumar, R. (1999). A correlational study between study habits and achievement in different school courses. *Indian Journal of Psychometry and Education, 30,* 53-56.

Washington, D.C. Cooperative Research Monograph, No. 2, U.S. Dept. of Health, Education & Welfare.

Weiner, B. (1986). *An attributional theory of motivation and emotion.* New York: Springer-Verlag.

Weiner, B. (1994). Integrating social and personal theories of achievement striving. *Review of Educational Research, 64,* 557-573.

Weinstein, R. (1989). Perceptions of classroom processes and student motivation: Children's views of self-fulfilling prophecies. In C. Ames & R. Ames (Eds.), *Research on motivation in education: Vol. 3, Goals and cognitions* (pp. 13-44). New York: Academic Press.

Weinstein, R.S., & Middlestadt, S.E. (1979). Student perceptions of teacher interactions with male high and low achievers. *Journal of Educational Psychology, 71,* 421-431.

Weist, M.D. (1997). Expanded school mental health services: A national movement in progress. In T.H. Ollendick & R.J. Prinz (Eds.), *Advances in clinical child psychology* (Vol. 19, pp. 319-352). New York: Plenum Press.

Wibrowski, C.R. (1992). *Self-regulated learning processes among inner city students.* Ph.D. dissertation, Graduate School of the City University, New York.

Williams, J. (1997). *School psychology: Its development and practice in the United States and its application in India.* (Monograph). Allahabad: SIEMAT.

Williams, T.H. (1972). Educational aspirations: Longitudinal evidence on their development in Canadian Youth. *Sociology of Education, 45,* 107-133.

World Bank (1997). *Development in practice: Primary education in India.* New Delhi: Allied Publishing.

Zimmerman, B.J. (1990). Self-regulated learning and academic achievement: An overview. *Educational Psychology, 25,* 3-17.

INDEX